Contents

Author's Note		iv
1	The Fog of War	5
2	The Golden Pavilion	9
3	Prince of Kamakura	25
4	Famine, Family and Favouritism	42
5	The Battle of the Kami Goryō Shrine	54
6	The First Year of Ōnin	60
7	Warriors from the West	73
8	The Second Year of Ōnin	86
9	The Bunmei War	100
10	The Road to Sengoku	108
Bibliography		119

Author's Note

In this book Japanese names are given in the conventional style of family name/clan name first, personal name second, for example Hosokawa Katsumoto and not Katsumoto Hosokawa. Note, however, that the personal name is normally used as the identifier in a textual narrative. So, for example, 'Katsumoto ordered an attack', not 'Hosokawa ordered an attack'. One other aspect of names is that I have chosen to sidestep the fact that many of the individuals noted here changed their names several times during their lifetimes. So, for example, the tenth Ashikaga shogun enters history as Yoshiki, changes his name to Yoshitada and finally becomes Yoshitane. For the convenience of my readers, I have called him Yoshitane throughout. Measurement of length, which appear in the sources as jō, shaku and sun, are given also in the metric system, while one shaku is almost exactly one foot in the imperial system. One jō is ten shaku and one sun is one-tenth of one shaku. The dates of events are expressed using the nengō (era name) for the year and the lunar calendar for the days, where, for example, 5m 3d means 'the third day of the fifth lunar month'. This is followed in brackets by a conversion to the western-style calendar.

This book is dedicated to Kerry, our border terrier, whose presence has brought us such joy during a difficult year and who has sat next to me during the writing of this book.

The Ōnin War 1467-77

A Turning Point in Samurai History

Stephen Turnbull

Helion & Company Limited
Unit 8 Amherst Business Centre
Budbrooke Road
Warwick
CV34 5WE
England
Tel. 01926 499 619
Email: info@helion.co.uk
Website: www.helion.co.uk
Twitter: @helionbooks
Visit our blog http://blog.helion.co.uk/

Published by Helion & Company 2021
Designed and typeset by Mary Woolley, Battlefield Design (www.battlefield-design.co.uk)
Cover designed by Paul Hewitt, Battlefield Design (www.battlefield-design.co.uk)

Text © Stephen Turnbull 2021
Photographs and illustrations © Stephen Turnbull 2021
Colour artwork by Giorgio Albertini © Helion & Company 2021
Maps by George Anderson © Helion & Company 2021

Every reasonable effort has been made to trace copyright holders and to obtain their permission for the use of copyright material. The author and publisher apologize for any errors or omissions in this work and would be grateful if notified of any corrections that should be incorporated in future reprints or editions of this book.

ISBN 978-1-914059-67-4

British Library Cataloguing-in-Publication Data.
A catalogue record for this book is available from the British Library.

All rights reserved. No part of this publication may be reproduced, stored in a retrieval system, or transmitted, in any form, or by any means, electronic, mechanical, photocopying, recording or otherwise, without the express written consent of Helion & Company Limited.

For details of other military history titles published by Helion & Company Limited contact the above address or visit our website: http://www.helion.co.uk.

We always welcome receiving book proposals from prospective authors.

1

The Fog of War

The Ōnin War of 1467–1477 has long been regarded as an important turning point in Japanese history. Indeed, in many books it is literally a turning point because, having read about the devastation that the conflict caused to Japan's capital city of Kyoto, the reader turns the page to be plunged immediately into the horrors of the one-and-a-half century long Sengoku Period, which took its name from the Warring States Period of Ancient China and arose from the collapse of central authority caused by the great civil war of Ōnin.

The name 'Ōnin War' is derived from Japan's traditional calendar system that uses *nengō* (era names), so its official title is in fact the Ōnin-Bunmei no Ran (The Ōnin-Bunmei War), because it took place during the two year-long Ōnin *nengō* and the first nine years of the Bunmei era that followed it. The term 'The Ōnin War' is nonetheless universally preferred for a decade of conflict which, according to the conventional view, was distinguished by its violence from a hitherto peaceful fifteenth century. In this scenario the Ōnin War acts as a portal to something even more terrible, and all else that is needed is to add the names of the rival participants who chose opposing sides when a succession dispute within the shogun's own family erupted into outright war. The two villains of the piece were Hosokawa Katsumoto (1430–1473) and Yamana Sōzen Mochitoyo (1404–1473), who launched a series of attacks on each other's mansions in Kyoto that succeeded only in destroying much of the city. The pleasure-loving shogun Ashikaga Yoshimasa gave up trying to control the situation, so the rival armies conducted virtual trench warfare across the city's blackened remains until their personal causes were exhausted. Even though both the original leaders died in 1473, the Ōnin War would drag on until its official end point of 1477. By that time the war had spread throughout Japan, and the sole claim to fame that could be enjoyed by Hosokawa Katsumoto and Yamana Sōzen was to have brought to an end a long period of stability when Japan had been blessedly free from the strife that had attended so much of her history.

This idea of the Ōnin War as a unique and meaningless tragedy that ended a peaceful age and led to a century of chaos has been around for centuries and has sometimes been expressed in almost apocalyptic terms.

THE ŌNIN WAR

In his *A History of Japan,* which was first published in 1910, Sir James Murdoch felt that towards its end the fighting of the Ōnin War had deteriorated into a stalemate on a 'chessboard of blackened ruins' and had become a 'Frankenstein' that its protagonists were unable to control. He then described the withdrawal of forces from Kyoto using the vivid language of 'the sky ruddy with the glare of the blazing cantonments'.[1] In 1961 George Sansom's *History of Japan* also saw the Ōnin War as a time of utter futility. 'Looking at the political scene against its background of flames and smoke one seems to see its actors as unfortunate creatures demented by their own ambitions'.[2] To such horrors may be added complete bafflement as to why the conflict started and what was really going on amidst the fog of war. In her 1994 book *The Culture of Civil War in Kyoto* Mary Elizabeth Berry found the events of the Ōnin War to be characterised by 'indeterminacy… discrete surprises… unresolved endings'.[3]

All these statements suggest that serious questions have still to be asked about the Ōnin War. First, there is some controversy over its exact dates, because so many related conflicts were occurring in different parts of Japan that it becomes difficult to determine when or where the episode conveniently labelled the Ōnin War began, or even when it properly ended. Thomas Conlan, who dares to put the term 'Ōnin War' within inverted commas in the title of a challenging article, suggests that the origins of the famous conflict lay with players outside the Hosokawa/Yamana axis, and that the deep involvement of the Ōuchi clan from Western Japan ensured that both the first and the last shots of the Ōnin War were fired not in Kyoto but far away in the vicinity of modern Hiroshima.[4] Conlan also extends the time frame in which the conflict should be understood, so that his suggested chronology for the Ōnin War gives its dates as 1465 to 1478.[5] There is also much confusion over the aims and outcomes of the war's individual battles, which are usually presented as irrelevant and meaningless affairs. For example, Paul Varley, whose partial translation of *Ōnin ki* (the chronicle of Ōnin) formed the basis of his classic study, felt that 'one battle is often indistinguishable from another', and reckoned that, 'the day to day fighting in Kyoto from 1467 to 1477 can be of little interest to anyone other than the military historian'.[6]

---

1 Murdoch, Sir James. 1925 *A History of Japan Volume I* (2nd Impression). London: Kegan Paul, Trench and Trubner, pp.616–617.
2 Sansom, George. 1961. *A History of Japan: 1334–1615.* London: The Cresset Press, p.228.
3 Berry, Mary Elizabeth. 1994. *The culture of Civil War in Kyoto.* Berkeley: University of California Press, p.13.
4 Conlan, Thomas D. 2020. 'The "Ōnin War" as the Fulfilment of Prophecy' *The Journal of Japanese Studies,* 46, 1, pp.31–60.
5 http://commons.princeton.edu/onin/ (Accessed 27 August 2020).
6 Varley, H. Paul. 1967. *The Ōnin War* (New York, Columbia University Press), pp.123–124.

THE FOG OF WAR

In this book I will demonstrate that these skirmishes were rarely just acts of random violence. There was a strategy lying behind both sides' moves in the Ōnin War, even if the events seem very confusing at first sight. That impression is partly due to the reliance that has traditionally been placed on the narrative of *Ōnin ki*, which is a *gunkimono* (war tale) with stylised battle descriptions and sometimes puzzling geographical descriptions. I shall make additional use of a number of diaries from the time which often contain eye-witness accounts of the events. This work will therefore endeavour to set the famous conflict in its correct military, historical and political context, explaining the war's origins, progress and outcome using a wide range of contemporary sources. I hope thereby to show that the Ōnin War was not a sudden irruption into an otherwise peaceful world or a unique tragedy within a peaceful century. It was instead a set of events that somehow became concentrated within Japan's capital city, a devastating combination that gave the Ōnin War an influence out of all proportion to the actual fighting that went on.

I shall also discuss developments elsewhere that were historical turning points in their own way, because in the years leading up to the Ōnin War several petty yet savage military encounters refused to be contained within their immediate areas, while violent peasants' revolts shook the ruling classes as much as any war could have done. There was also a siege that became the longest in Japanese history up to that time and resulted in the execution of two children, and as for the leading protagonists in the Ōnin War being from the Yamana and Hosokawa clans, the highly influential Hatakeyama family were engaged in a succession dispute that had been going for ten years before the Ōnin War began and was not resolved until 1499. Japan had also experienced the premeditated murder of the reigning shogun, and all these events happened to a background of famines, droughts and floods that killed more people than any of the battles ever did.

Crucial to my reconstruction of the events of the Ōnin War has been the identification of place names, a matter that is sometimes difficult because certain temples, for example, share names with better known institutions

A mounted samurai wielding a *naginata*, the popular pole arm used both from horseback and on foot at the time of the Ōnin War.

that lie in other areas of the city or are places that have been relocated since the Ōnin War. I would therefore like to thank everyone who has helped me in the preparation of this book, including in particular, my guides to the sites in Kyoto. These places include the Kami Goryō Shrine where the first battle took place, the site of the shogun's 'Palace of Flowers' and the locations of the rivals' urban fortresses. These former mansions were positioned surprisingly close together, and it requires no great leap of the imagination to envisage the bustling modern avenue of Horikawa-dōri as it once was: an area of no-man's land where arrows flew between lookout towers and rocks were launched by catapult over a riverbed and a deep, body-filled ditch.

My trip also took me far from Kyoto to the former capital of Kamakura and the old provinces of the Kantō that now lie on the outskirts of modern Tokyo. Here stand monuments, graves and battle sites which remind us that a parallel war was fought in Eastern Japan by the shogun's deputies, and here too clans like the Hōjō would soon take advantage of the chaos and forge kingdoms of their own in what we now call the Sengoku Period when they were free from interference by the shogun, whose authority had been diminished as never before by the terrible yet much misunderstood Ōnin War.

2

The Golden Pavilion

There may be differences of opinion over when and where the Ōnin War actually began but, even if the reality of Japan's political situation for much of the fifteenth century was that of sporadic and petty civil wars, our story has to start somewhere, and I trust that the reader will forgive me if I start with a battle. The encounter in question is the fierce battle of Uchino that was fought in 1391. It lasted only one day and was almost the sum total of the events that made up the Meitoku no Ran (the Meitoku War or the Meitoku Rebellion). Like the battle of the Kami Goryō Shrine that would provide the curtain raiser for the Ōnin War a few decades later, the battle of Uchino was fought in the heart of Kyoto, but this is not to suggest that its importance lies in the fact that armed encounters in the capital were limited to these two instances. Far from it, Kyoto had changed hands at least eight times during the past half century, and almost all those exchanges had involved bitter fighting and the destruction of property.

The significance of the battle of Uchino is that it was conducted within a period of time defined by an old war while belonging conceptually to a new war in a very different age. The new era would be characterised by armed opposition to shoguns and culminated in the Ōnin War. The ongoing conflict, which was moving swiftly to its close, had involved armed opposition to emperors. That was the Nanbokuchō War – the War Between the Courts – which owed its origins to the attempt by Emperor Go-Daigo (1288–1339) to re-establish the same power and hegemony that former emperors had enjoyed in earlier centuries.

Go-Daigo, who ascended the throne in 1318, spent many years pondering the achievability of a true imperial restoration. It was a daunting task, because for a very long time his sacred predecessors had been forced to occupy a role that was largely ceremonial. Since 1192 the real power in the land had been exercised by the Bakufu, the 'government behind the curtain' (the name was based on the curtains that traditionally surrounded a general's field headquarters in battle) exercised by the shogun. His title meant 'the barbarian-suppressing commander-in-chief' and defined succinctly the dictatorial role which had been permanently delegated to the incumbent by ancient imperial commission. The original order had fallen upon Minamoto Yoritomo (1147–1199), the first shogun of the Minamoto dynasty, but after two generations Yoritomo's descendants' right to rule was usurped by his wife's relatives from the Hōjō family. By the fourteenth century the Hōjō, who ruled as Regents from the Bakufu headquarters in Kamakura, had become sufficiently unpopular for the young and vigorous Emperor Go-Daigo to raise troops against them and make real his dream of an imperial restoration.

Go-Daigo's revolution was launched in 1331 and, (initially at any rate), was a dismal failure. The ambitious young emperor was captured and forced into exile on a remote island, but two years later he returned in triumph and his loyal armies overthrew the Hōjō in crucial battles at Kyoto and Kamakura. Yet in spite of his victories Go-Daigo's dream of true imperial rule was not to be realised. It turned out instead that the forces his rebellion had unleashed had merely led to the replacement of one dynasty of shoguns by another, and the new variety – the Ashikaga Bakufu – were no more inclined to accept genuine imperial rule than the Hōjō Regents had been. In 1336 Go-Daigo was again forced to flee from Kyoto and took refuge in the mountains of Yoshino. That was the beginning of the 'War Between the Courts' because Go-Daigo's descendants would rule from a succession of temporary palaces in Yoshino as the so-called 'Southern Court' in opposition to the 'Northern Court' who were located in Kyoto's imperial palace and were supported by the Ashikaga family.

It had been the decision of the first Ashikaga shogun Takauji (1305–1358) to move the Bakufu headquarters to Kyoto after a century and a half in Kamakura and make the shogun's capital the same as that of the emperor, and because many of the events that took place over the following century occurred in or around Kyoto it is worth spending a little time describing the overall layout of the city and its long history.

Kyoto is a comparatively modern name for the city that was replaced as Japan's capital in 1868 by Tokyo. It is located within a horseshoe of forested mountains that opens on to a flat plain on its southern side, where a number of rivers merge in an area called Yawata before draining ultimately into Osaka Bay. Kyoto had become the new capital of Japan in the year 794 to replace Nara and the short-lived Nagaoka as the seat of the emperor. The new settlement was called Heian-kyō, the 'capital of peace and tranquillity'. It was laid out in a checkerboard pattern of intersecting streets and city blocks in imitation of the former capital of the Tang Dynasty of China, just as Nara had been. The overall layout has survived to this day in spite of the addition of modern highways, and many of the old street names can still be identified where they once formed dusty thoroughfares between the walls of temples, mansions, commercial premises and commoners' houses.

Eighth century Heian-kyō had been designed along a north to south axis entirely to the west of the Kamo River. A broad avenue (its course is the modern Senbon-dōri) had as its northern apex the Daidairi or Great Palace Enclosure. At its southern end lay the main entrance to the city through the massive gate called Rashomon that was made famous by the title of the classic Kurosawa movie. Parallel to the central avenue lay ran eight others,

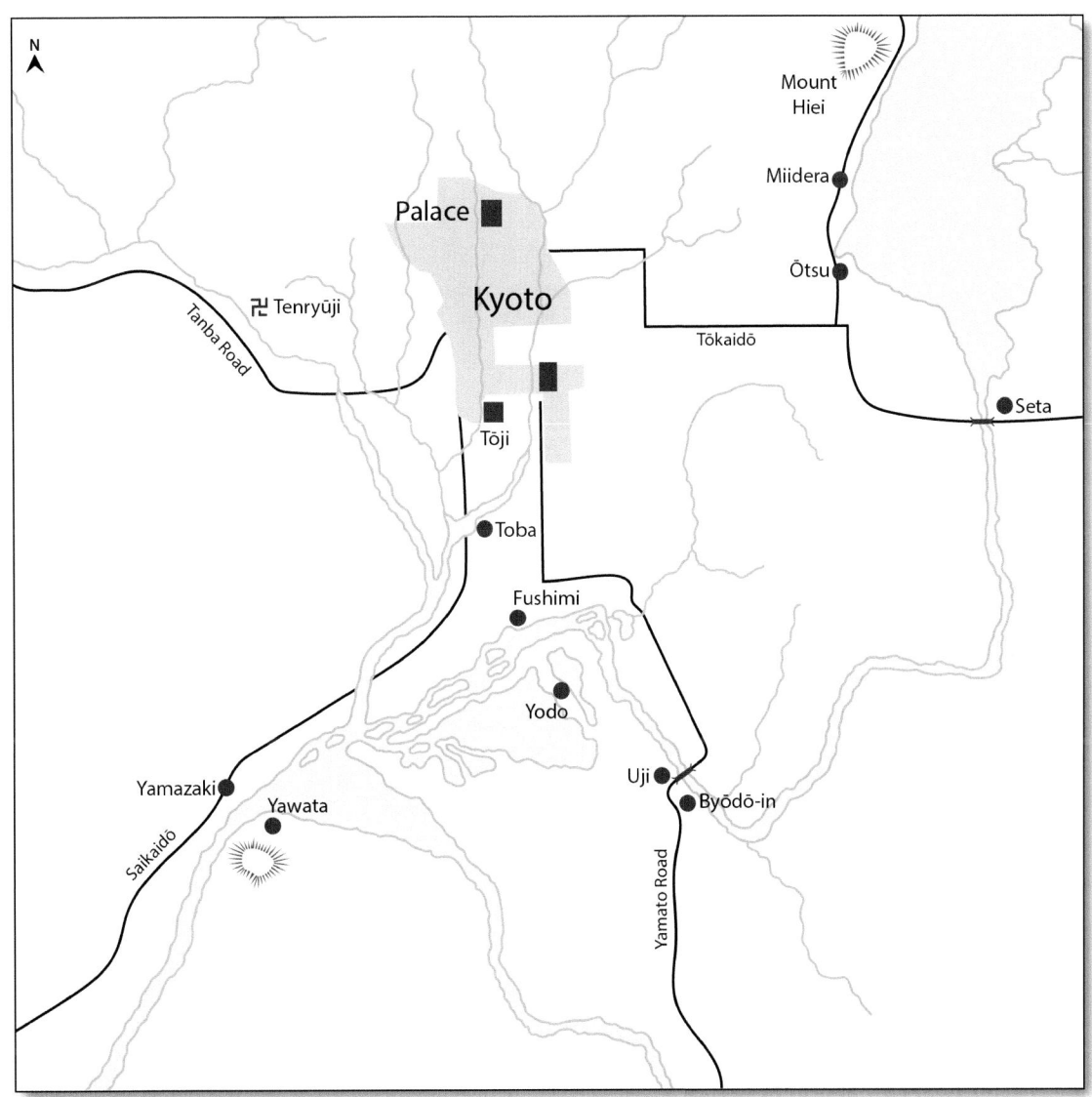

Kyoto and its environs in the fifteenth century, showing the confluence of rivers in the Yawata area that provided an outer defence for the city.

THE ŌNIN WAR

which were crossed by a number of east to west streets, the most important of which were the nine *jō* known by the numbers 1 to 9 from Ichijō in the north to Kujō in the south. These intersecting thoroughfares delineated city blocks that ideally had regular square sides of 1 *chō* (120m) in length and were walled around. The larger ones held a single palace, mansion or temple complex within their boundaries; others were further divided into smaller lots for commercial premises or commoners' dwellings. The Daidairi Palace lay between Ichijō and Nijō.

The imperial court had stayed in Kyoto when Minamoto Yoritomo set up his Bakufu in distant Kamakura in 1192, and although its political influence was thereby greatly diminished, the Kamakura Period had allowed Kyoto to become a major centre of Buddhism and a very important commercial crossroads. Known variously then as Miyako or Raku, the city flourished, and its layout now developed around an east to west axis with a northern half (Kamigyō) and southern half (Shimogyō). When Ashikaga Takauji brought his Bakufu back to Kyoto Kamigyō became the aristocratic quarter and Shimogyō became the domain of the townspeople. The northern border of Shimogyō changed from time to time but was usually reckoned as being Nijō, while the city's hub of commercial activity was located around Shijō. In 1378 the shogun's palace was moved to an area adjacent to the north-south avenue called Muromachi, hence the usual name of the Muromachi Period for the era between the years 1336 and 1568 when the Ashikaga clan held supreme authority under the emperor and ruled from Kyoto.

The site of the Hana no Gosho (Palace of Flowers) is marked by this memorial stone in the grounds of the Daishōji in Northern Kyoto. The Palace of Flowers was the headquarters of the Ashikaga Bakufu and was twice as large as the imperial palace.

The greatest change of location within Muromachi Kyoto happened in respect of the imperial palace, for which there had been no permanent site since the year 1228 when the original Daidairi, which had fallen into disrepair, became uninhabitable after a fire. The site was then abandoned and would become known as Uchino ('the inner field'): the location of our first battle. A small fragment of the grounds survives today as a public park. In 1337 Ashikaga Takauji settled the emperor of the Northern Court in a private residence called Tsuchimikado. When the two courts were united in 1392 the place attained the status of palace (*gosho*) and has retained its location to the present day, although the extensive grounds of what is now called Kyoto's Old Imperial Palace are much more extensive than was allotted to it during the fourteenth century, because the shogun's own palace, the Hana no Gosho or 'Palace of Flowers', exceeded it in size twice over.

By the year 1391 the War Between the Courts was moving mercifully to its close. The exiled Southern Court had been losing support for years and many people of influence were starting to believe that a settlement between the two dynasties was in sight. There was still some fighting to come, but in practical terms any military actions that now arose in the name of the Southern Court against the reigning shogun – a statesman who of course owed his position to the Northern Court – tended to be little more than excuses for the exercise of personal ambitions and the discharge of grievances. Nevertheless, the continued existence of the Southern Court, militarily impotent though its supporters increasingly were, meant that there was still an emperor around on whose behalf a rebel could be said to be acting. Based on that argument one's rival – even the Ashikaga shogun himself – could be declared an enemy of the court: an appellation that

The third Ashikaga shogun Yoshimitsu (1358–1408) represents the Ashikaga dynasty at its best and set the benchmark of greatness from which his ancestors would tragically fall. A leader in war and also a statesman, Yoshimitsu commissioned the famous Golden Pavilion in the hills of Kitayama.

still carried some weight when it came to enlisting outside support for a supposedly righteous cause. This state of affairs lasted well into the fifteenth century, and at late as 1469 the Yamana faction in the Ōnin War sought out a descendant of the last Southern Emperor to give their side the same imperial legitimacy as their rivals.

In 1391 the ruling shogun was the third to come from the Ashikaga dynasty. He was called Ashikaga Yoshimitsu (1358–1408) and had been installed as shogun in 1369 at the tender age of eleven, so he had ruled under a Regency for some time. History has tended to treat Yoshimitsu kindly. He is warmly remembered for restoring foreign relations with China after the Mongol Invasions and for developing international trade, but he is above all credited with being the peacemaker whose wise rule ended the Nanbokuchō War and established the situation of stability that is supposed to have ended so tragically during the First Year of Ōnin. Comparisons with those latter days are valid on several points, and it can be argued in many ways that Ashikaga Yoshimitsu represents the Ashikaga dynasty at its best because he was the ruler who set the benchmark of greatness from which his ancestors would tragically fall. Yoshimitsu was also a supreme patron of the arts who commissioned the Kinkakuji, the glorious Golden Pavilion in the hills of Kitayama to the west of the shogun's palace.

In political terms Yoshimitsu was probably the Ashikaga shogun who best achieved a working balance between his own centralised authority and that of his *shugo* or military governors. These were the men chosen from the shogun's chief vassals to govern the shogun's realm within the provinces to which they were assigned. In some provinces the post of *shugo* moved from one family to another; in others the continuation of the post within one family led to long-lasting and serious succession disputes. Theoretically, a *shugo* was chosen on the basis of his ability to govern and not as a reward for service or simply to curry favour, but during the Nanbokuchō War many *shugo* had taken advantage of both the political confusion and the benefits of loyal military service to establish their own proprietorial bases. It was partly for this reason that the early Ashikaga shoguns began to require the *shugo* from the central provinces to reside within Kyoto where the shogun could keep an eye on them. Their number consisted of around twenty at any time and in total they had jurisdiction over forty-five provinces. On Kyushu its *shugo* were accountable to the shogun's deputy for the island, and in the east the *shugo* were under the jurisdiction of the shogun's deputy in Kamakura, a post that would cause several headaches, as the following pages will demonstrate.

The residential requirements for the central bloc of *shugo* was envisaged as a way of preventing major wars. It was by no means the aristocratic hostage system that would characterise the later Tokugawa Bakufu during the seventeenth century although, just as would happen under the Tokugawa, forced residence in a splendid mansion within the boundaries of Kyoto was by no means an unpleasant experience. The culture of the capital could be enjoyed to the full, financial and commercial interests could be pursued, and the system also allowed the *shugo* endless opportunities for what we

THE GOLDEN PAVILION

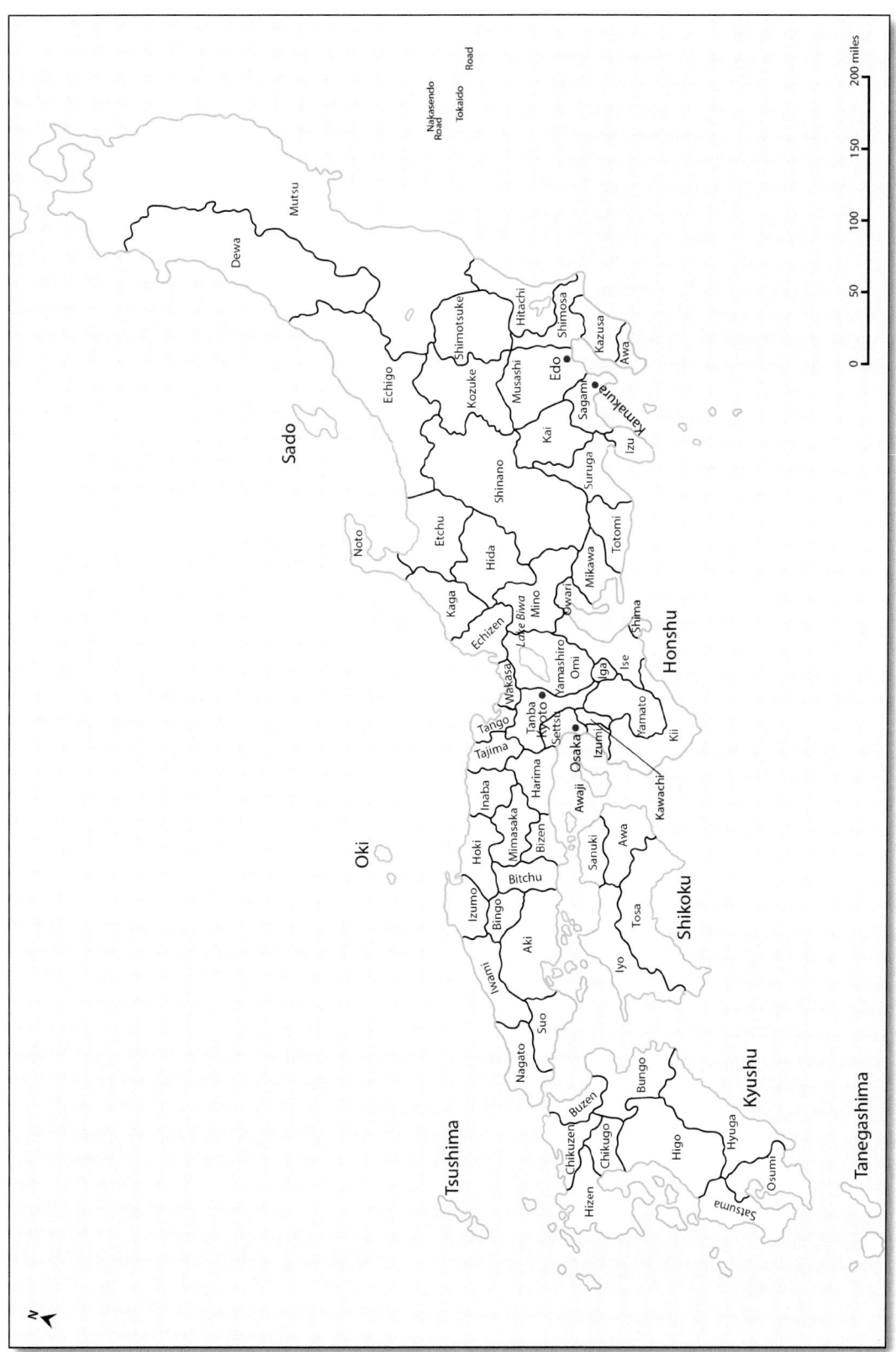

The provinces of Japan, showing the locations of Kyoto, Edo and Kamakura.

would now call networking. As a result, the *shugo* who resided in the capital were very supportive of the Bakufu during the reign of Yoshimitsu and his immediate successors. Things changed after 1441 when the ruling shogun was murdered in the horrific incident to be described later. Their presence in the capital then proved to be problematic at many levels, the most serious of which was the fact when the Ōnin War started Kyoto became its main battleground. There was some fighting out in the provinces, but otherwise the *shugo* confronted each other from defensive bases that had once been luxurious mansions, now converted into urban fortresses with ditches and watchtowers.

Linked to this factor of the urban proximity of future rivals was the existence of a handful of key families who held the greatest influence over the shogun. Three in particular – the Shiba, Hosokawa and Hatakeyama – alternated occupancy of the post of Kyoto Kanrei: the shogun's deputy in the capital. Along with other grandees they also made up the *yoriai* (the council of chief vassals) and the *samurai-dokoro* (the board of retainers) who represented the shogun's authority in military and police matters. Yet just as the *shugo* were acquiring seemingly more power over the shogun through these positions, so they were also threatened by the growing influence of the *shugodai* (deputy *shugo*) on whom they themselves relied on to administer the provincial estates that the *shugo* themselves rarely if ever visited.

The other crucial role of the *shugo* was to provide troops in the shogun's service. Ashikaga Yoshimitsu took an active interest in military matters and commanded a personal guard, but a shogun would otherwise rely on provincial troops marshalled by the *shugo*. Ashikaga Yoshimasa, the shogun of the Ōnin War, took no more interest in military matters than he did in anything else other than his own pleasures, so the loyalty (or otherwise) of the *shugo* mattered more than ever before. The system was therefore unstable. As Thomas Conlan sums up so well, 'The post of *shugo* became the fulcrum of provincial power and the basis for regional organisation, and yet the concentration of power inherent in this office served to destabilise Japan'.[1]

The Meitoku Rebellion

All these problems with *shugo* lay blessedly in the future during the year 1381, when Ashikaga Yoshimitsu's aesthetic and political influence received a major boost by a visit to the Palace of Flowers from Emperor Go-En'yū. The enjoyable event lasted six days and gave legitimacy to Yoshimitsu's cherished vision of the shogun's palace as a place where the military and

---

[1] Conlan, Thomas D. 2010. '*Instruments of Change: Organisational Technology and the Consolidation of Regional Power in Japan, 1333–1600*', in Ferejohn, John A. & Rosenbluth, Frances McCall (Eds.). *War and State Building in Medieval Japan*: pp.124–158. Stanford: Stanford University Press, p.141.

imperial nobility might come together. Yoshimitsu also undertook a number of stately visits of his own. On the face of it these trips were to visit famous religious sites, but they were also a way of cultivating friendships and creating strategic alliances should the need ever arise, as it would in 1391 and 1399 when Yoshimitsu's programme of developing loyal networks paid handsome dividends by helping him to quell two serious rebellions. The revolts were led by protagonists who bore family names that would reappear during the Ōnin War, and Ashikaga Yoshimitsu took an active part in the military operations against them.

Yoshimitsu's role as a leader in war is much less well known than his statesman-like achievements, but he needed both skill-sets to counter two important incidents that were notable for the threats they posed to Kyoto. The first of the conflicts was the Meitoku Rebellion and our introductory battle of Uchino. In some ways it was the last battle of the Nanbokuchō War, but in many other ways it was the start of something new, because up to that point Yoshimitsu had managed to manipulate rival *shugo* so well that they policed and, in some cases, destroyed themselves. That had been the outcome in the case of a dispute within the Toki family early in 1390, when one faction of the family who were loyal to the shogun obligingly did away with the rebellious faction who were not so inclined.

The Meitoku War was different. Its instigator was a rich *shugo* called Yamana Ujikiyo (1344–1391), who had served the Ashikaga dynasty with great loyalty for many years, not only by fighting the armies of the Southern Court during the Nanbokuchō conflict but by punishing recalcitrant members of his own relatives at the shogun's behest. For this he and his immediate family had been richly rewarded. By 1391 the Yamana controlled eleven provinces out of Japan's total of sixty-six and were thus nicknamed the *roku bun no ichi dono*: 'the lords of one-sixth'. This meant that in spite of their service record, the Yamana posed a theoretical threat to the Ashikaga, who sought to curtail their rapidly increasing powers. Thus, it was that in the eleventh lunar month of the Third Year of Meitoku Yamana Mitsuyuki was deprived of his control of the

Yamana Ujikiyo (1344–1391) served the Ashikaga dynasty with great loyalty for many years but then instigated the Meitoku Rebellion. He was killed at the battle of Uchino in 1391.

province of Izumo. The pretext was that he had illegally seized imperial property.

When Mitsuyuki objected to this course of events Ashikaga Yoshimitsu ordered his loyal followers to teach the Yamana a lesson, but the Yamana clan rallied rapidly behind their leader. Ujikiyo and Mitsuyuki decided to strike pre-emptively and persuaded their brother Yoshimasa to raise an army in his own province of Kii. Yamana Ujiie, another nephew of Ujikiyo, also left Kyoto to raise an army from his own estates. Ujikiyo then petitioned the Southern Emperor to have the Ashikaga family declared enemies of the throne. Needless to say, Ashikaga Yoshimitsu had already done the opposite and labelled the Yamana as rebels through the offices of the Northern Emperor, but with the silver brocade banner of the rival Southern Emperor as his standard, Ujikiyo and Mitsuyuki marched on Kyoto.

Ashikaga Yoshimitsu took personal command of his troops and reviewed them at the mansion of his loyal supporter Isshiki Akinori. The author of *Meitoku ki* (the *gunkimono* that relates the events of the rebellion) takes pains to inform his readers how the shogun was attired that day and the reasons for his choice of costume. Over his courtier's attire of a *kosode*, a courtier's padded silk robe with an *eboshi* (stiffened cap), Yoshimitsu wore a suit of armour, but it was not an elaborate *yoroi*, just a plain black leather *haramaki* such as would have been worn by a humble samurai, to make the point that he was the subject of the Court and was also supremely confident of subjugating his enemies in the name of the rightful emperor.[2]

The shogun's army took up a position at Uchino, the empty space in the heart of Kyoto where centuries before had stood the Daidairi palace. By this time the 2,000 strong army of Yamana Mitsuyuki had arrived at the temple of Ninnaji out to the West, while two separate columns under Yamana Ujikiyo and Yamana Takayoshi had crossed the Katsura River and were approaching the fields of Uchino from the South. Yoshimitsu's first line of defence was a shield wall erected by his loyal follower Ōuchi Yoshihiro (1356–1400), who bore the brunt of the first Yamana assault. A hail of arrows greeted their advance, at which Ōuchi Yoshihiro counter-attacked and swept them to one side after two hours of fierce fighting. He reported his success to Ashikaga Yoshimitsu, who presented Yoshihiro with a sword as a reward.

Meanwhile the two other detachments under Yamana Mitsuyuki and Ujikiyo had joined forces in the vicinity of Nijō and Ōmiya. Here they were confronted by more of the shogun's forces and the fighting was fierce. It only went Yoshimitsu's way following the intervention of his own Horse Guards who were led into battle, it would later be claimed, by the shogun himself. Yamana Ujikiyo, the leader of the rebellion, was killed during this phase of the contest. *Meitoku ki* describes how Yamana Kojirō, a youth of seventeen, went to help his fallen master Ujikiyo, referred to here as Ōshū:

---

2   *Meitoku ki* in Hanawa Hokiichi. 1912. *Gunsho Ruijū* Vol 13 (1912 edition) (Tokyo), p.244.

He cut down two enemy horsemen. But on realising that he himself would also be killed, Kojirō galloped up to share in the honour of death. Ōshū's last prayer came to his ears, but then the assembled enemy struck. Ōshū saw them approach from the side, but Ōshū was speedily overcome and his head taken and raised on high. Without thinking about what to do, Kojirō threw himself down from his horse's back while holding his sword and flung himself across Ōshū's corpse, brandishing his blade, but Kojirō too was overcome, and holding tight on to Ōshū's shoulder guard he cut his own belly.[3]

The overall casualty list at Uchino was 879 dead on the Yamana side and 164 among the shogun's defenders.[4] The rebel leader Yamana Ujikiyo would eventually be buried in front of a temple which Yoshimitsu established in Kyoto to prevent any of the dead Yamana from turning into that most terrible of things: an angry ghost seeking spiritual revenge. His nephew Mitsuyuki fled back across the Katsura River and headed for the safety of Tanba Province. He would later shave his head and became a priest, but he was put to death in 1395 with his rebellious spirit still unquenched.

Out of the surviving members of the Yamana family Ujiie was allowed to keep Inaba Province, while two members of the next generation of the Yamana: Tokihiro and Ujiyuki, hung on to Hōki and Tajima respectively, having sworn loyalty to the shogun. Otherwise, within two months of the Meitoku Rebellion eight out of the eleven Yamana provinces had been re-allocated to generals loyal to the Ashikaga who had performed bravely at the battle of Uchino, although certain stubborn members of the family needed considerable military pressure before they relinquished their domains. For example, the provinces of Izumi and Kii were granted to Ōuchi Yoshihiro because of his brave service at Uchino, but their owner Yamana Yoshimasa would not surrender his domains until Yoshihiro had destroyed his key fortresses.

Soon only remnants of the Yamana hegemony now remained, and in the end the personal retainers of the late Yamana Ujikiyo took a stand along with a few stubborn Southern Court sympathisers at a very poignant location: the castle of Chihaya, the mountain fortress where the famous Kusunoki Masashige had held out at the start of the Nanbokuchō War half a century earlier. The Ashikaga armies attacked and destroyed their army in a quick and symbolic victory that challenged the very idea that the Southern Court still had to be taken seriously as rivals. The military success at Chihaya also prompted shogun Ashikaga Yoshimitsu to send Ōuchi Yoshihiro to enter into secret negotiations with the Southern Court and finally end the war that had now become almost irrelevant. The proposal that Yoshihiro would put forward was that the Northern and Southern lines should in

---

3   *Meitoku ki*, p.261.
4   *Meitoku ki*, p.268.

THE ŌNIN WAR

future alternate when the succession became vacant. For the time being the reigning Northern Emperor would be regarded as the legitimate ruler to whom the crown jewels should be speedily handed over, while the heir of the Southern Emperor would be proclaimed Crown Prince. An agreement was reached, and at a short ceremony within the temple of Daikakuji in 1392 a long and bitter era finally came to an end.

The Ōei Rebellion

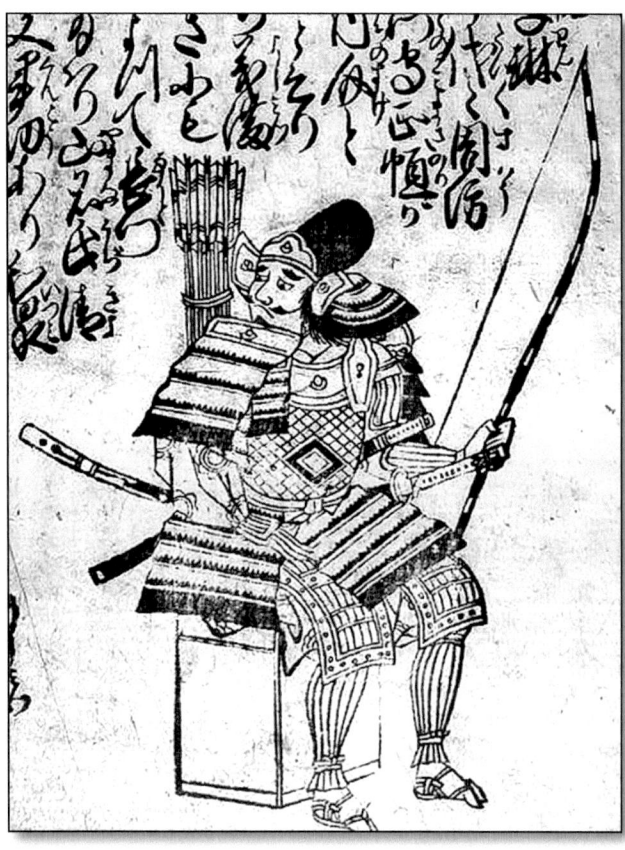

Ōuchi Yoshihiro (1356–1400) was richly rewarded for his service during the Meitoku Rebellion but then went on to conduct a revolt of his own known as the Ōei Rebellion. He was killed during the siege of Sakai in January 1400.

In 1394 Ashikaga Yoshimitsu ceased to reign as shogun and formally passed the responsibilities on to his son, but it is perfectly clear that he continued to rule behind the scenes for many years, so his abdication must not be regarded as an abandonment of personal responsibility. In some ways his retirement was a guarantee of a peaceful transition in the event of Yoshimitsu's death, because his successor would be already in post. Whatever his motives, it was still Yoshimitsu who confronted in person the last and greatest military challenge of his reign: the Ōei no Ran (Ōei Rebellion) of 1399–1400. It was led by a former hero of the Meitoku Rebellion, because after the defeat of the Yamana the only serious political challenge that Yoshimitsu faced was from Ōuchi Yoshihiro, who now controlled six provinces. Just as in the case of the Yamana, all this wealth and influence in the hands of one strong man put Yoshimitsu on his guard, and when Yoshihiro's rebellion began the Bakufu was ready for him.

The immediate stimulus for Ōuchi Yoshihiro's revolt is supposed to have been his resentment at being required to pay towards the building of the Kitayama Palace and its Golden Pavilion. The construction began in 1397 and all the *shugo* were expected to contribute to the enormous cost. Yoshihiro had objected, saying that warriors should serve the shogun with bows and arrows rather than money, but it is likely that he had been planning his revolt for years. Yoshihiro's strength lay in the support of other western *shugo* and the wealth that had come his way through sometimes illicit trade. Yet even after lodging his protest at the levy Ōuchi Yoshihiro stayed sufficiently loyal to the shogun to obey Yoshimitsu's subsequent command to chastise his enemies in Kyushu, but when Yoshihiro's younger brother Mitsuhiro fell in battle and no order was given to reward the man's father for the tragic loss, relations between Yoshihiro and his shogun deteriorated still further.

The story of Yoshihiro's revolt is told in the *gunkimono* called *Ōei ki*, which has the ominous subtitle of 'The Destruction of Ōuchi Yoshihiro'. Having disobeyed several requests to go to Kyoto and explain his behaviour, probably on the not unreasonable grounds that he might be assassinated, Yoshihiro began to conspire with others. The Southern Court, officially at any rate, no longer existed, so Yoshihiro sought a risky alliance with Ashikaga Mitsukane (1378–1409), the shogun's deputy in Kamakura who ruled eastern Japan on Yoshimitsu's behalf. He also made alliances with local lords who had been adversely affected by Yoshimitsu's past policies, including Yamana Tokikiyo, the eldest son of the late Yamana Ujikiyo.

After refusing to obey Yoshimitsu's latest command to present himself in Kyoto Yoshihiro withdrew to the port of Sakai in Izumi Province to make military preparations for an attack on the capital. Much alarmed, Yoshimitsu sent a trusted adviser to arrange a peaceful settlement to the dispute, but Yoshihiro announced that he would be marching against Kyoto along with Mitsukane's army from Kamakura. With Yoshihiro so obdurate and the risk that support from Kamakura might not be a bluff, Yoshimitsu knew that he would have to attack at once. He set up camp at the temple of Tōji and then advanced to Yawata in the southeast of Kyoto, where the confluence of several rivers provided a natural barrier against any threat to the capital from that direction. There he was joined by two representatives from his loyal Kyoto deputy families: Shiba Yoshimasa and Hatakeyama Motokuni.

Back in Sakai Ōuchi Yoshihiro held a council of war with his generals. His trusted adviser Sugi Bungo-no-Kami advocated leaving their headquarters and taking the army by sea to launch an attack against the shogun's temporary base at Yawata, but defensive advice prevailed, and Yoshihiro hurriedly began fortifying Sakai on an elaborate scale. The resulting fortifications were very impressive for the end of the fourteenth century. Those were typically the days of the *yamashiro*, elaborate mountain castles in remote locations, so the enclosure of a prominent port with defences resulted in the battle of Sakai becoming something unusual in Japanese history: a siege of a fortified town. Judging by the *Ōei ki* descriptions of the defence works, the harbour of Sakai must have been encased within a wooden square consisting of a threefold timber parapet with enough space between each layer to allow freedom of movement for mounted men while being covered from above by archers. The three outer walls on the landward sides were entirely surrounded by a 1.8 km long moat that touched the sea at either side. The triple parapets were further defended by 48 large lookout towers (*seirō*) which were about 7 *jō* (22 metres) tall, together with 1700 smaller *yagura* (literally 'arrow towers'). The four sides of the city were divided into twelve defensive sections of 16 *jō* (almost 50 metres) in length, each of which was identified by a wooden gate and a bridge across the moat on the landward sides.

THE ŌNIN WAR

Yagura (towers) like this one at the reconstructed site of Arato Castle formed a major part of the defences of Sakai during the Ōei Rebellion. They allowed the observation of an enemy and acted as defensive structures from which arrows and stones could be discharged.

Yoshihiro boasted that the enemy could not defeat him at Sakai 'even if they brought up one million men'.[5] For a month his bragging appeared to be true, and Yoshihiro's confidence was further bolstered when two of his allies conducted daring operations against the besieging forces from other directions. Both moves gave great heart to the defenders, although neither was successful in influencing the ultimate outcome of the rebellion. The first was a raid by Yamana Tokikiyo against Kyoto from Tanba Province. The operation did some damage to the capital and caused great alarm to its citizens, but when Tokikiyo attacked the shogun's base at Yawata he was forced to withdraw.[6] The second raid occurred when Kyōgoku Hidemitsu advanced on Kyoto from the direction of Ōmi Province, but he was held up by the warrior monks of Miidera.[7]

Ashikaga Yoshimitsu launched his first attacks on the walls of Sakai on 11m 29d [26 December 1399] at the Hour of the Hare (6.00 a.m.) while pirates from Shikoku and Awaji blockaded the harbour with a fleet of more than 100 ships. The author of *Ōei ki* notes the dreadful noise that emanated from their war cries and the banging of war drums as the shogun's army hit the parapets from all sides. As one example of the action, we note that in the northern sector Hatakeyama Motokuni broke through two layers of defences but was held up at the inner wall where arrows and stones were rained down upon his men.[8] Sugi Bungo-no-Kami led a counterattack after it had grown dark. Meanwhile the Hosokawa and Akamatsu troops had been attacking from the south and other contingents had moved in from the east. The first day's fighting lasted well into the night, at which both sides withdrew to rest.[9]

---

5   *Ōei ki* 8 at http://muromachi.movie.coocan.jp/oueiki/oueiki08.html (Accessed 19 June 2020).
6   *Ōei ki* 12 at http://muromachi.movie.coocan.jp/oueiki/oueiki12.html (Accessed 19 June 2020).
7   *Ōei ki* 13 at http://muromachi.movie.coocan.jp/oueiki/oueiki13.html (Accessed 19 June 2020).
8   *Ōei ki* 9 at http://muromachi.movie.coocan.jp/oueiki/oueiki09.html (Accessed 19 June 2020).
9   *Ōei ki* 10 at http://muromachi.movie.coocan.jp/oueiki/oueiki10.html (Accessed 19 June 2020).

From Ōuchi Yoshihiro's point of view, merely to have driven off the shogun's army was a victory, and when repeated attacks over the next few weeks produced no further results Ashikaga Yoshimitsu realised that something drastic would be needed. His army accordingly began preparing huge versions of the wooden torches (*sagichō*) that were used at fire festivals during New Year celebrations. Each torch was made from bamboo and brushwood and was long enough to be stood up on its end and then dropped across the moat to fall against the outer walls of Sakai. The chosen date for the attack had to be postponed because of rain, but eventually at the Hour of the Hare on 12m 21d [17 January 1400] hundreds of lighted torches were dragged and toppled into place. The moment was well chosen, because a strong south-easterly wind was blowing, so the flames quickly raced up the towers and began to consume the wooden defences.[10]

Within the fortifications those who had been fighting from the *yagura* fell into the midst of the flames and were burned to death. As the battle proceeded, the fire spread from the *yagura* and the *seirō* on all four sides until the morning, so that the whole 10,000 *chō* area of Sakai was burned out, illuminating the blue sky above while blood flowed into the ocean.[11]

When the flames began to leap from one layer of his defences to the next Ōuchi Yoshihiro and his followers realised that there was no honourable alternative open to them other than an heroic death in battle. Yoshihiro accordingly left Sakai by one of its northern gates and attacked Hatakeyama Mitsuie, the son of Motokuni, until only thirty of Yoshihiro's companions were left alive. Soon only one was spared, and when he too fell Ōuchi Yoshihiro was left alone in the melee as a long sword blade slashed into his nose and mouth.[12] He was soon confronted by Hatakeyama Mitsuie, to whom he cried out, 'I am Ōuchi Yoshihiro the greatest warrior under Heaven. Kill me now and take my head for the shogun to see'. He then committed suicide on the field of battle and Mitsuie took his head.[13] On learning

An example of a large wooden torches (*sagichō*) that are used at the Kurama Fire Festival in Kyoto. Torches like these were dropped against the wooden defences of Sakai to set them on fire.

---

10 *Ōei ki* 14 at http://muromachi.movie.coocan.jp/oueiki/oueiki14.html (Accessed 19 June 2020).
11 *Ōei ki* 20 at http://muromachi.movie.coocan.jp/oueiki/oueiki20.html (Accessed 19 June 2020).
12 *Ōei ki* 17 at http://muromachi.movie.coocan.jp/oueiki/oueiki17.html (Accessed 19 June 2020).
13 *Ōei ki* 18 at http://muromachi.movie.coocan.jp/oueiki/oueiki18.html (Accessed 19 June 2020).

that his master Ōuchi Yoshihiro had died, the loyal Sugi Bungo-no-Kami achieved a death that was almost as spectacular:

> [He] cut his way into the midst of the great enemy in the northern side, confronting and cutting down six of the enemy on the way. He was a very strong man who used an *ōdachi*, and without any thought for his own life among the madness of death he discarded his *tachi* and began his attack, and over 200 horsemen retreated about 2 *chō* as if they were leaves scattered in a storm. Yamana Nyūdō drew his own *tachi* and moved towards Bungo-no-Kami in order to engage with him. At this, Bungo did not miss the opportunity but thrust at him with his long sword, which pierced him through his breastplate and went out at the rear. Nyūdō tried to pull Bungo towards him in order to stab him to death, but Bungo had already ruled out that possibility by transfixing him with his long sword and, after staggering back about 10 *shaku*, Nyūdō died where he stood.[14]

Sugi Bungo-no-Kami then cut his own way into a dense crowd of enemies and died fighting as the Ōei Rebellion came to its end.

Ashikaga Mitsukane, the shogun's deputy in the east, was on his way from Kamakura when he heard of Yoshihiro's defeat, so he prudently withdrew. Mitsukane then apologised to the shogun and was forgiven for his rebellious thoughts, so it turned out that Ōuchi Yoshihiro's Ōei Rebellion was the final challenge that Yoshimitsu would face during his long and successful reign. The triumphant shogun was now able to continue the process he had already begun of establishing political control and expressing it partly through aesthetic means. Yoshimitsu was a great supporter of Zen Buddhism and established the temple of Shōkukuji next door to the Palace of Flowers, but the construction of a private mansion for himself among the western hills of Kitayama in imitation of the palace of the emperor would provide the everlasting symbol of his age. The Kinkaku or Golden Pavilion is the only building left standing within the temple grounds today. The first floor once contained a statue of Amida along with an image of Yoshimitsu himself. The second floor contained a statue of Kannon and was used occasionally for social gatherings, while the top storey was square in shape and was a Zen sanctuary. In 1408 Emperor Go-Komatsu visited Yoshimitsu at his Kitayama estate. This imperial blessing was the culmination of the recognition that Yoshimitsu had always cherished, but within a month the great shogun died, leaving as his legacy a chain of political achievements and the concrete symbol of his age that is the glorious Golden Pavilion.

---

14   *Ōei ki* 19 at http://muromachi.movie.coocan.jp/oueiki/oueiki19.html (Accessed 19 June 2020).

3

Prince of Kamakura

Reference was made in the previous chapter to Ōuchi Yoshihiro seeking support from Ashikaga Mitsukane, the shogun's deputy in Kamakura in 1399. As the focus of the present chapter will be that important office of state, it is worth taking a closer look at the nature and relevance of the Kamakura post.

The background to the establishment of the Kantō Kanrei, i.e., Deputy for the Kantō area (which encompasses modern Tokyo and the ancient provinces round about), lies in 1335 when the first Ashikaga shogun Ashikaga Takauji chose to set up his new Bakufu in the imperial capital of Kyoto. Fearful of creating a power vacuum in the East, Takauji appointed his son Yoshiakira (1330–1367), the future second Ashikaga shogun, as Kantō Kanrei. When Yoshiakira became shogun, he was succeeded as

The Daibutsu (Great Buddha) of Kamakura still gazes down on the city just as it did when the East of Japan was ruled by the Kamakura Kubō on behalf of the shogun. Rivalry between successive shoguns and the headstrong Ashikaga Mochiuji (1398-1439), was to have enormous consequences for almost forty years.

THE ŌNIN WAR

Kantō Kanrei by his younger brother Ashikaga Motouji (1340–1367), after which the position became hereditary within Motouji's junior branch of the Ashikaga family. Its powers grew to be so extensive that the office became known as the Kamakura-Fu: the 'Kamakura Government', and later in the fourteenth century the title of Kantō Kanrei was changed to the better-known appellations of Kantō Kubō or Kamakura Kubō. It was a significant change of title, because Kubō was an honorific court title that denoted an official equivalent to a prince.

During the early fifteenth century the incumbent 'Prince of Kamakura' became a source of anxiety to the Bakufu in Kyoto, and matters were not helped by the fact that the Kamakura Kubō had his own deputy, for whom the previous title of Kantō Kanrei was resurrected. The newly labelled position became hereditary within the Uesugi clan and would be responsible for even more confrontation, because the Kantō Kanrei was appointed by the Bakufu rather than being chosen by the Kamakura Kubō himself. The result was that, far from ensuring that the Kantō area was tranquil, the system was very unstable. Over the following century various princes of Kamakura tried aggressively to further their own interests, leading to a number of incidents in the east of Japan akin to the Meitoku and Ōei disturbances that had happened in Kyoto.

The most serious period of dissension began around the time of the accession of the fourth Ashikaga shogun Yoshimochi (1386–1428). He had ruled in name as shogun since the great Yoshimitsu had retired, but it was only when his father died in 1408 that Yoshimochi was able to experience the full responsibilities of office, to which a long-lasting challenge would be supplied by the incumbent Prince of Kamakura, Ashikaga Mochiuji

The Tsurugaoka Hachiman Shrine in Kamakura was the site of many important events during the time of the Muromachi Bakufu including the suicide of Uesugi Zenshū, who revolted against his master the Kamakura Kubō in 1417.

(1398–1439), a violent and ambitious man whose independence of thought and deed were to have enormous consequences for almost four decades. Trouble started in 1415, when the increasingly presumptive Mochiuji severely criticised his chief advisor: the Kantō Kanrei Uesugi Zenshū (?–1417). Mochiuji goaded the latter into a serious rebellion that ended with Zenshū's army smashing their way into the Kamakura palace, taking over the city and forcing its haughty prince to flee to the mountains.

The Bakufu had some sympathy with Zenshū's plight in the face of Mochiuji's outrageous behaviour, but they could not in any way support a revolt against their deputy in the east and were forced to send an army to reinstate Mochiuji. Zenshū's forces were driven back through a snowstorm to commit suicide in Kamakura's Tsurugaoka Hachiman shrine. Mochiuji was then safely reinstated in post, but the shogun decided to keep a watchful eye on him. This proved to be a very wise move because, on the pretext of hunting down surviving sympathisers of Zenshū, Ashikaga Mochiuji carried out a purge of anyone who dared to challenge him, particularly those who owed their positions to the Bakufu and not to his own patronage.

The Lottery Shogun

Following the death of Uesugi Zenshū in 1419, Uesugi Norizane (?–1466) became Kantō Kanrei and a further round of mistrust began between the two leading officials in Kamakura, but matters would deteriorate even more rapidly with the death of shogun Ashikaga Yoshimochi in 1428. Like his father before him, Yoshimochi had abdicated in favour of his son, but when the young Yoshikazu (1407–1425) died after scarcely two years as the

Ashikaga Yoshinori (1394–1441) was nicknamed the Lottery Shogun because he was chosen by a priest drawing lots at the Iwashimizu Hachiman Shrine. He proved to be a tyrant and was assassinated by one of his rivals in 1441.

fifth Ashikaga shogun his father took office for a second time. Yoshimochi had no other natural heirs, so when he died in 1428 urgent discussions were held as to who should replace him as shogun. Ashikaga Mochiuji, the Prince of Kamakura, felt very strongly that he should be the one to succeed, but his past behaviour had certainly not endeared him to the Bakufu, who decided instead to choose a candidate from one of the late shogun's four younger brothers. Unfortunately, all of them had renounced the secular life for the Buddhist priesthood, and as none immediately presented himself as suitable shogun material, Yoshimochi's advisors sought divine help and drew lots for the succession at the Iwashimizu Hachiman shrine. The deity's choice was a monk at Kyoto's Shōren-In who was the current Chief Priest of the Tendai Sect. On the day after the death of his brother he came blinking into the sunshine of Japanese politics as the sixth Ashikaga shogun Yoshinori (1394–1441).

The god's decision to choose Yoshinori would eventually prove to be a disaster for the House of Ashikaga. On the positive side Yoshinori's reign would be shown to have sustained, and even in some cases increased the power of the Bakufu in ways that greatly benefited his successors. The revival of trade with China lies also to his credit, but all of Yoshinori's achievements came at a terrible price, because in accepting the 'Lottery Shogun' (as he would scornfully be termed), the Bakufu had unknowingly acquired a tyrant. One by one Yoshinori's opponents both sacred and secular felt the force of his wrath in a mixture of incidents that veered from the terrible to the comic. At the latter extreme lies his anger when the crowds watching a cockfight prevented Yoshinori's procession from passing by. As a result, Yoshinori not only banned cockfighting but ordered that no one in Kyoto should keep chickens. Yoshinori is also supposed to have ordered the assassination of Hino Yoshisuke, a prominent courtier, and was also prone to terrorise his servants for minor misdemeanours such as serving food which he did not like. At the more serious end lay his enmity against the influential Akamatsu Mitsusuke (1381–1441). Three of Mitsusuke's ladies-in-waiting, one of whom was his own sister, had been put to death in 1432 on the shogun's orders for some misdemeanour. Soon it was Mitsusuke's turn to be arrested, but he escaped to his estates in Harima Province, which Yoshinori then attacked in vain.

Yoshinori's reign also begun badly in an entirely different sphere, although the blame for it could not be entirely laid at his door, because the year 1428 saw the first example of an *ikki*, a phenomenon that would return time and again to plague successive shoguns. The word *ikki* has two meanings: an uprising or riot, and the league, confederacy or simply the mob (depending upon the formality of the organisation) that was conducting it. The 1428 example is known as the Shōchō no Tsuchi-Ikki, the 'Land Uprising of the year of Shōchō'. Incursions of this sort would accelerate in the years leading up to the Ōnin War and became an almost annual experience until being properly repressed from about 1512 onwards. The prefix *tsuchi* (land) that was given to the 1428 revolt referred to a belief that the rioters were all workers of the land. In fact, the uprising seems to have included all those residing in a particular agricultural location from the local gentry the *jizamurai* downwards, because in those days there was little practical distinction between warriors and farmers at the lower levels of society. Writing later in *Daijōin jisha zōjiki*, the monk Jinson noted to his horror that it was the first time since the founding of Japan that an uprising of commoners had ever occurred.[1]

The year 1428 saw the first example of a *tsuchi-ikki*, an uprising by rural dwellers demanding the cancellation of debt. The rioting caused great damage in Kyoto and shocked the Bakufu. Here farmers are shown armed with makeshift weapons.

---

1   Sansom, George. 1961, p.208.

THE ŌNIN WAR

The immediate cause of the 1428 *ikki* was the poor harvest of the previous year, a consequent spread of famine and a nasty 'three-day disease' (probably cholera) which had caused the rioters' lives to become intolerable. Many of the insurgents were also suffering from considerable burdens of debt: an indication of an economic change that had recently taken place within the home provinces, where loans had become important as agriculture grew more commercialised. Much of the lending was provided by rich institutions such as temples and wealthy *sake* brewers in the city, so these moneylenders became a prime target for the rioters. Some commoners in Kyoto who were themselves in debt may also have joined in the scuffles, so the lines of demarcation between the invading outsiders and the peaceful city dwellers were by no means clear cut. Their numbers are also likely to have been swelled by poorer city inhabitants who had emigrated to the capital when famine occurred, because it was not uncommon for starving people to flock to Kyoto as *rumin* (vagrants) to seek relief.

The immediate instigators of the 1428 *tsuchi-ikki* would appear to have been the influential *bashaku* of Ōmi Province, the teamsters whose packhorses provided overland transport. Although of modest economic means, their vital logistical role meant that they were perfectly capable of seriously disrupting the delivery of rice and other products to Kyoto. Thousands of suffering farmers from the area quickly joined the *bashaku* and poured into the capital, destroying storehouses, burning loan records, seizing pawned goods and demanding above all that the Bakufu should issue an edict cancelling all obligations to repay debts. The uprising was therefore also referred to as the first *tokusei-ikki*. *Tokusei*, which literally means 'virtuous rule', implied that the government should exercise the virtue it possessed by cancelling crippling debts using an act of grace.

The Hoso Jizō in Yagyū village has an inscription carved into it confirming the pledge of debt cancellation made to the *tsuchi-ikki* in 1428 by their local landowner, the temple of Kōfukuji in Nara.

The 1428 *ikki* set a pattern of violence that would grow depressingly familiar for many decades to come. The rioting that took place to the southeast of Kyoto was so bad that the Bakufu had to send in several hundred troops to quell the disturbances, and the eleventh lunar month saw three weeks of mayhem within Kyoto itself. Nara experienced very similar upheavals that took in some great monasteries to whom many farmers were in debt. A few months later in 1429 a 'copycat' *ikki* took place in Harima Province against its landowner Akamatsu Mitsusuke to the slogan of 'no samurai in the province'. The samurai in question were the Akamatsu retainers, so Mitsusuke was forced to withdraw troops from Kyoto to quell the unrest in his home territories.

In the event no debt-cancelling edict was issued by the Bakufu as a result of the chaos in Kyoto, but as most of the written records referring to monies owed had been destroyed in the riot the *ikki* members had achieved their *tokusei* by a different route. Other institutions did however comply with their demands, and the influential temple of Kōfukuji in Nara was one such organisation. It made binding pledges of debt cancellation, one of which was carved into the side of a stone monument at Yagyū village and still exists to this day as a memorial of those tumultuous events.

The 1428 *tsuchi-ikki* shook the Bakufu's authority, but greater damage was caused to Ashikaga Yoshinori's personal reputation when the monks of Mount Hiei fell foul of the shogun in an incident that set him directly against the Buddhist establishment. Mount Hiei lies to the northeast of Kyoto from where, according to very ancient beliefs, it protected the capital against evil. The monastery of Enryakuji that lay on its summit had been richly endowed for centuries by a succession of emperors and shoguns and was the foremost Buddhist university in Japan. Before his accession Yoshinori had been the head priest of the Tendai Sect of which Enryakuji was the centre, and appointed his own younger brother in his stead when he became shogun. A dispute in 1434 led to a riot by the monks of the Enryakuji, whom Yoshinori subdued with considerable violence in an astonishing lack of sympathy.

The monks, however, had friends in high places, and in the following year of 1435 Yoshinori heard about alarming rumours that were circulating among them that his great rival — the Kamakura Kubō Ashikaga Mochiuji — had placed a curse

Enraged at being passed over for the post of shogun, the Kamakura Kubō Ashikaga Mochiuji presented a petition at the Tsurugaoka Shrine cursing shogun Yoshinori. It is supposed to have been written, or at the very least sealed, in his own blood.

THE ŌNIN WAR

upon him. The rumours turned out to be true because, buoyed up by reports of Yoshinori's tyrannical behaviour, Mochiuji's thoughts had changed to rebellion against the man who had been chosen as shogun instead of him. In a dramatic gesture Mochiuji had visited the Tsurugaoka Hachiman Shrine in Kamakura and presented a petition written in his own blood. It has been preserved to this day, and reads:

> My petition, here on Tsurugaoka, before the likeness of the Divine General Kongō, is for continued luck in war; the prosperity of my descendants; that the present second generation will live at ease, and above all for a curse to last for one hundred million years upon my sworn enemies who place burdens on those who serve the Kantō; this I pray.[2]

Yoshinori's immediate reaction was to attack the messengers, so he sent troops in a further raid against Mount Hiei and had several high-ranking prelates beheaded. The defiant monks retreated inside Enryakuji's Main Hall, and as Yoshinori's army approached them, set fire to their refuge, burning it to the ground and immolating themselves within. This stunning act of suicidal defiance sent shock waves through the Buddhist establishment, and so furious was Yoshinori at the reaction to it that he forbade anyone even to talk about the incident at Enryakuji or face decapitation. That this was no idle threat is confirmed by an entry in the court diary *Kammon*

The rebuilt Konpon Chūdō, the main Buddha Hall of the Enryakuji on Mount Hiei, where defiant monks immolated themselves rather than surrender to the army of Yoshinori.

---

2   Minegishi, Sumio. 2017. *Kyōtoku no Ran*. Tokyo: Kōdansha, p.45.

Nikki whereby a tea merchant who talked about the immolation on Mount Hiei was overheard and beheaded on the spot. The diarist ends his note with the words 'Everyone is afraid. Say nothing, say nothing.'[3]

The Eikyō Rebellion

For a reigning shogun to be declared the enemy of Buddhism was bad enough, but Yoshinori also had many human enemies, and throughout his reign he faced no fiercer rival than Ashikaga Mochiuji, the embittered Prince of Kamakura. Eastern and Western Japan were now controlled by strong, self-willed and ruthless men who hated each other, and Mochiuji had never forgiven the Bakufu for failing to choose him as shogun. The expression 'sworn enemies' which he had used in his Blood Petition at the Tsurugaoka Shrine referred directly to Yoshinori and his tyranny, but the Prince of Kamakura was hardly above blame for the situation. As noted earlier, he had never been on good terms with his deputy Uesugi Norizane. When a minor squabble broke out in 1436 between two petty lords in Shinano Province one of them asked Mochiuji for armed support, but Norizane insisted that the Prince of Kamakura should not get involved in such a dispute nor be seen to be aiding one loyal retainer of the shogun against another. At first Mochiuji bowed before this reasonable advice, but the following year he rejected his deputy's counsel and took sides in the quarrel. It was then rumoured that he intended to kill Norizane under cover of the disorder, so the latter fled to his estates.

A fragile peace would eventually be made between the two Kamakura grandees, but in 1438 they fell out again over the coming-of-age ceremony of Mochiuji's son. Mochiuji had chosen the adult name of Yoshihisa for the boy, but Uesugi Norizane pointed out that it was against all precedent to select for one's son an adult name containing a syllable of the shogun's name without having sought prior permission. The ceremony went ahead nonetheless and Mochiuji's son became Ashikaga Yoshihisa, but Norizane was now so fearful for his life that he dared not visit the

Uesugi Norizane (?–1466) became Kantō Kanrei in succession to Uesugi Zenshū and faced the wrath of Ashikaga Mochiuji for many years to come. When Kamakura fell to the shogun's forces Norizane pleaded for Mochiuji's life. The plea was ignored and Mochiuji committed suicide. Norizane then became a monk and lived the rest of his life as a renowned scholar.

---

3   As quoted in Ishinomori, Shōtarō. 2017a. *Dōmin, Bakufu wo yurugasu*. Tokyo: Chūōkoronsha, p.92.

Kamakura palace for fear of assassination. He withdrew instead to an ally's fortress, and when he heard that Mochiuji had sent an army to hunt him down, the hapless Uesugi Norizane asked the Bakufu for armed help.

That was the incident that finally forced the Bakufu to reel in their unruly Kamakura representative, but the first military action against Mochiuji in the quelling of what would be called the Eikyō no Ran proved disastrous. The shogun's army marched eastwards from Kyoto under the imperial banner with a commission from the emperor to chastise an enemy of the throne. On 9m 10d [29 September 1438] the shogun's army divided into two. One unit began to cross the Pass of Hakone. Mochiuji's local supporters set up a position in a spot that was particularly dangerous for an invading army. They lined up their shields and lay in wait:

> The western side of the Hakone Mountains is a precipitous and deeply cut valley and the cliffs are tall, so you can see the enemy, but they cannot see your positions. The soldiers defended it like wild beasts and would send their archers forward in turns to fight, so that even tens of thousands of enemies would find it impossible. However, the attackers were a large army, and the defenders were few, so they said, 'How long can this mountain hold us up?'. Before the attack the invaders were supremely confident of victory, so all 500 horsemen dismounted, and using their shoulder plates as a defence against arrows and lining up the tips of their swords and *naginata*, they climbed up to attack in one mad rush.[4]

Ashikaga Mochiuji's army had a secret weapon. *Eikyō ki* identifies it by using the word *ishiyumi,* which had two ancient meanings. The first indicated a stone-firing crossbow, a weapon that had not been used for hundreds of years, but *ishiyumi* also meant a simple contrivance whereby large rocks that were too heavy to be lifted and thrown by hand were hung by ropes from a stockade's walls. They were placed in position prior to an attack being launched and were secured through a loophole to a stout foundation of some sort. The rope would be cut by a well-timed sword stroke so that the heavy missile fell on to the attackers. It is therefore easy to imagine a large number of rocks being tied in place on the cliffs overlooking the pass with smaller ones simply piled up, ready for the Bakufu army's advance. As they clambered up the slopes:

> ...the local Hakone unit released their *ishiyumi* all in one go. Many tens of thousands of troops were sent flying by this, and a tide of humanity fell down one on top of another into the deep valley bottom. Few of them may actually have been directly destroyed by

---

4   *Eikyō ki* 5 at http://muromachi.movie.coocan.jp/eikyouki/eikyouki05.html (Accessed 25 June 2020).

the enemy, but the number killed by being pierced through by their own swords or naginata is impossible to gauge.⁵

Wounded by the stones and from their own weapons, the invaders were trapped by the dense undergrowth at the edge of the pass. They were then cut down like sitting ducks so that, 'for four or five months after the battle, blood still clung to the wild grass, and dead bodies were strewn across the highway'.⁶

Fortunately for the Bakufu's cause, those advancing by the Ashigara Pass made much better progress and achieved total surprise against Mochiuji's forces:

> …raising their war cries, they galloped into the midst of the great army without giving them any time to loose arrows in reply… They were struck from all sides, dyeing red the grass of the fields, while the sweating horses kicked up the gore, and the water of the river was stained with the blood from the corpses of the common soldiers that were obstructing its flow.⁷

The dramatic act of suicide by the last Kamakura Kubō Ashikaga Mochiuji.

Meanwhile Uesugi Norizane's army had successfully driven off the force sent by Mochiuji and were advancing towards Kamakura. Formerly loyal generals now began to desert the Prince of Kamakura and changed sides to the Bakufu. Unable to place any hindrance in their way, Mochiuji withdrew to his palace where he tried to buy time and his personal survival by swearing an oath of obedience to the shogun. The merciful Uesugi Norizane responded in a positive vein and pleaded with Yoshinori that Mochiuji's surrender should be accepted, that he should be made to retire to a monastery and that his son Yoshihisa should become the new Kamakura Kubō. But the shogun was intent upon vengeance and ordered Uesugi Norizane to hunt down Mochiuji, who had now taken refuge in the temple of Eianji. During the second lunar month of 1439

---

5 *Eikyō ki* 5 (Accessed 25 June 2020).
6 *Eikyō ki* 5 (Accessed 25 June 2020).
7 *Eikyō ki* 5 (Accessed 25 June 2020).

Norizane, much against his own inclinations, launched an attack on the Eianji and Ashikaga Mochiuji, the last prince of Kamakura, committed suicide. His son Yoshihisa followed suit in soon afterwards.

The siege of Yūki Castle

Not long after the death of Ashikaga Mochiuji, Uesugi Norizane renounced the world and became a priest. He passed the post of Kantō Kanrei on to his younger brother Uesugi Kiyokata, on whose shoulders now fell the unpleasant business of completing the subjugation of those who had been involved in Mochiuji's Eikyō Rebellion. Kiyokata's attention was focussed on the Yūki family of Shimōsa Province, who provided a refuge within Yūki Castle for Ashikaga Mochiuji's three surviving sons. Yūki Ujitomo realised that this merciful gesture could put his family at odds with the Bakufu and very likely lie them open to attack, so he gathered together his leading followers to consider their position:

The mausoleum of Ashikaga Mochiuji in the grounds of the Betsuganji in Kamakura.

Although our family is not particularly famous, we have never been disloyal throughout all our generations. No one in the Kantō has ever spoken ill of us, so our young men can be relied upon. During the rebellion last year we had peaceful negotiations with the shogun and both he and Uesugi Kiyokata trust us, so do we want to go back on this?... Please consider the matter carefully...

Four of the clan elders cut off their pigtails as a sign of renouncing the world. Among them only Mizutani Ise-no-Kami said, after much deliberation, 'To abandon a fight is not in accordance with the Way of Bow and Arrow. I can't do it'. So, he went back to the castle while the other three retired to their mansions.[8]

The split within the Yūki ranks was somewhat made up for by a surge in support from other local prominent families, and from provinces far and near the former followers of the Kamakura Kubō and many unemployed *rōnin* who had lost their masters in the war ensconced themselves inside Yūki Castle. There they set up extensive siege works in preparation for what would turn out to be the longest siege in Japanese history up to that time. It began during the third lunar month of 1440 and lasted an entire year before the final attack was launched.

---

8   *Eikyō ki* 11 at http://muromachi.movie.coocan.jp/eikyouki/eikyouki11.html (Accessed 26 June 2020).

PRINCE OF KAMAKURA

The inner moat of Yūki Castle, which withstood the longest siege in Japanese history up to that time. As supporters of the late Kamakura Kubō the Yūki family faced an onslaught from the Bakufu.

Part of the reason for the long siege was that Yūki Castle was garrisoned by a large army who had ample supplies of food and water. *Eikyō ki* says that they had 10,000 *koku* of rice, an amount that would theoretically feed 10,000 men for one year. Yūki Castle was also built in a naturally defensible area on a modest hill that dominated the flat rice lands of the Kantō round about. A small river, the Tagawa, flowed round its northern and eastern sides some distance away and joined the Kinugawa a few kilometres to the south-east. The besiegers set up siege lines three *chō* (about 300 metres) distant from the castle's wooden parapets. Within that gap lay two extensive ditches between which were strewn a wide abattis of felled trees, but which side carried out these works is not clear. They would certainly have benefited the garrison in the event of an attack, but from an enemy's point of view they also served to isolate Yūki Castle still further from outside support and any further supplies.

Observation towers were set up in front of the main besieging commanders' positions, just as had been done against Sakai in 1399, and *Eikyō ki* claims that these ones were massive constructions of 10 *jō* in height, which would make them the same as the largest ones recorded later for the Ōnin War. The siege lines consisted of either a two-or three-fold fence depending upon the precise location. *Yūki Senjō Monogatari*, a further *gunkimono* about the campaign, notes the defenders setting up towers of their own and defending them with *ishiyumi*: 'On top of the steep embankments were *ishiyumi* with ropes through wooden tubes that when cut through would fall'.[9] Flags of the Yūki and their allies flew in defiance from the rammed earth rampart and 'every day the sound of the bows and

---

9   *Yūki Senjō Monogatari* in Hanawa Hokiichi. 1912. *Gunsho Ruijū* Vol 13 (1912 edition) (Tokyo), pp.729 & 730.

arrows and the war cries echoed between the Four Deva Kings above and the netherworld at the deepest depths of the earth'.[10]

There were many casualties during the subsequent skirmishes, but neither side attempted to engage in any decisive manner, and instead settled down to glare at each other from within their defence lines, 'so the time passed to no purpose'.[11] With that the winter came to its end, and the stimulus for the conclusion of the siege was the discovery by the besiegers that food supplies within the castle were beginning to run out:

> On 4m 15d [5 May] Kiyokata turned to his generals and said, 'In ancient times it was not unheard of for enemy castles to resist for two or three years, but that was when there were only 500 or 1,000 horsemen. In the present case, half of Japan is here and for many months we have besieging this one castle causing trouble for the local people, and in addition those back in Kyoto are growing impatient. If we leave things as they are it will bring eternal shame upon our future generations, Tomorrow is a lucky day, so let's have a full scale attack'.[12]

The final attack began on the 'lucky day' of 4m 16d [6 May 1441]. When the assault started the defenders tried to move the three sons of Ashikaga Mochiuji to a place of safety, but the older two were apprehended as they fled. The weakened garrison were unable to resist the subsequent onslaught and when Kiyokata succeeded in setting fire to the outer defences Yūki Ujitomo decided to die honourably in a suicidal charge. 'Because the garrison had long been resolved to die, they did not hesitate but plunged into the midst of the great army... The horses galloped into the enemy without stopping, while countless riderless horses became dyed red and knocked down enemies scattered under their hooves.'[13] To the south of the castle at the rear of the siege lines was a mound that the besiegers had chosen as a command post and named the Sashiki-tsuka ('reviewing mound').[14] It became the target for Yūki Ujitomo's suicidal move out of the castle. He and his son led the attack through the enemy lines and then disembowelled themselves on the hillock. When the survivors of the garrison tried to escape from the burning castle they were driven into the river and many thousands more were killed.

---

10   *Eikyō ki* 13 at http://muromachi.movie.coocan.jp/eikyouki/eikyouki13.html (Accessed 26 June 2020).
11   *Eikyō ki* 13 (Accessed 26 June 2020).
12   *Eikyō ki* 5 at http://muromachi.movie.coocan.jp/eikyouki/eikyouki05.html (Accessed 26 June 2020).
13   *Eikyō ki* 5 (Accessed 26 June 2020).
14   *Yūki Senjō Monogatari*, p.730.

PRINCE OF KAMAKURA

The besiegers' command post during the siege of Yūki Castle was called the Sashiki-tsuka (reviewing mound). It became the target for Yūki Ujitomo's suicidal move out of the castle when the fortress fell and now contains the battle memorial.

The shogun Ashikaga Yoshinori was delighted by the successful conclusion to the long siege of Yūki, and was determined that the power of the princes of Kamakura should be broken forever. Mochiuji and his eldest son Yoshihisa were already dead, so the two younger captured princes, Haruō, aged fifteen and 12-year-old Yasuō, were put to death. The severed heads of the defeated defenders of Yūki Castle were displayed in Kyoto, and with that the Eikyō Rebellion came to an end.

The two young sons of Mochiuji, Haruō, aged fifteen- and 12-year-old Yasuō, were put to death after being captured at Yūki Castle.

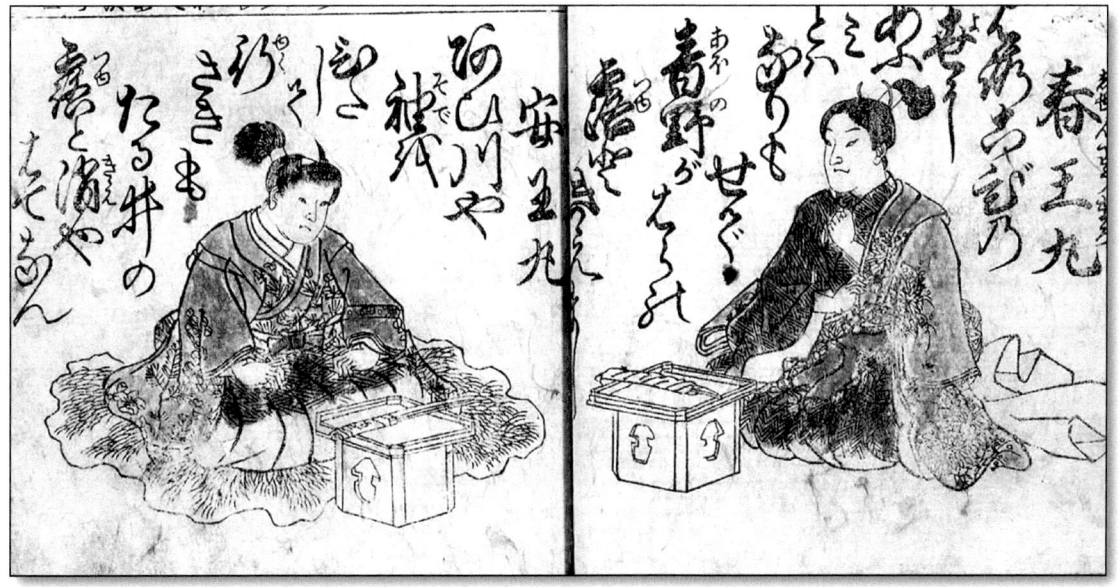

39

THE ŌNIN WAR

The Kakitsu Incident

The quelling of the Eikyō Rebellion was the greatest triumph that the 'Lottery Shogun' would ever enjoy, but terrible retribution was soon to come his way, because among the other long-standing targets of Yoshinori's enmity had been the family of Akamatsu. They were a clan with a fine pedigree and roots in the province of Harima. During the early days of Go-Daigo's imperial restoration they had played a major role in capturing Kyoto from the Hōjō in 1333. However, as it was with so many others, when their rewards for sacrifice proved to be paltry the Akamatsu embraced Ashikaga Takauji's rebellion against Go-Daigo and became fervent supporters of the Northern Court. This meant that they had backed the winner, so the family grew in status and wealth through its service to the Ashikaga Bakufu. In 1391 the Akamatsu added Mimasaka Province to their domains following the defeat of the Yamana at the battle of Uchino.

Akamatsu Mitsusuke (1381–1441) succeeded to the family headship in 1427, but shogun Yoshimochi enraged them when he sought to bestow Harima Province on his favourite, a kinsman of theirs called Akamatsu Mochisada. The affair ended with the suicide of Mochisada, but history was to repeat itself in the succeeding generation when Mochisada's son Sadamura became a favourite of shogun Ashikaga Yoshinori. In 1441 intelligence reached the ears of Akamatsu Mitsusuke that Yoshinori was planning to deprive him of Harima, Bizen and Mimasaka and transfer them to young Sadamura. To prevent this happening, Mitsusuke took the drastic step of having the shogun murdered, although this was so unusual a course of action that other factors are likely to have been involved.

The remarkable incident happened as follows. During the sixth lunar month of 1441 a messenger arrived at the shogun's palace requesting the pleasure of his company at the mansion of Akamatsu Mitsusuke. Within its extensive grounds there was a pond where ducklings had recently hatched, so Mitsusuke invited the shogun to come and see the ducklings swimming while enjoying a celebration of the Bakufu's glorious victory at Yūki Castle. Suspecting nothing – his

Akamatsu Mitsusuke (1381–1441) is shown here as a villain in the kabuki theatre. In the Kakitsu Incident of 1441 he arranged for shogun Yoshinori to visit his mansion to celebrate the victory at Yūki Castle. Horses were set free from the stable and in the ensuing confusion the shogun was murdered.

entourage was tellingly small – shogun Ashikaga Yoshinori arrived at the Akamatsu mansion on 6m 24d of the First Year of Kakitsu [12 July 1441]. The ducklings were delightful; the festivities were lavish; the *sake* flowed freely and a performance of the *sarugaku* dance drama *Ukai*, which told the story of the murder of a cormorant fisherman, was mounted in the shogun's honour. But as the main actor in the drama approached the shogun a great commotion was heard. Mitsusuke's horses had broken out of their stables and had entered the garden. The gates were quickly closed, ostensibly so that the horses could be brought under control, but this was merely to provide cover for a brutal assassination, because the armed guards who appeared on the scene took no notice of the stampeding horses and instead attacked the shogun. Two men grabbed him from behind while another sliced off his head. Some of Yoshinori's defenceless attendants were cut down; others escaped the carnage by climbing over the walls.

So perished the Lottery Shogun Ashikaga Yoshinori, who was struck down 'like a dog' in a brutal assassination known to history as the Kakitsu Incident. Writing centuries later the unsympathetic historian Arai Hakuseki (1657–1725) blamed the evil Yoshinori's inevitable fate on the perverse decision made all those years earlier of choosing a shogun by drawing lots. In his *Tokushi yoron* of 1712 he wrote scathingly:

> How could the deity of the Iwashimizu Shrine let such a man bring suffering to the people, even by making him lord of the empire for a single day? If the god had any intelligence at all, that would never have happened. If the god didn't exist, what folly it was to consult him, before doing one's best oneself. So, it was the greatest fortune for the Ashikaga family and for the Japanese people that Yoshinori was killed when he was.[15]

Whether or not the deity of the Iwashimizu Shrine could be blamed for the mistake, the murder of the shogun had totally changed Japan's political scene and marked the beginning of the decline of the Muromachi Bakufu. The leadership it had once exercised would never be the same again, its erosion accelerated by a shift in the balance of power between shogun and *shugo* that would come to its ultimate fruition in the Ōnin War.

---

15 Ackroyd, Joyce (Trans.). 1982. *Lessons from History: Arai Hakuseki's Tokushi yoron* St. Lucia: University of Queensland Press, p.244.

4

Famine, Family and Favouritism

Yamana Sōzen Mochitoyo (1404–1473), nicknamed 'The Red Lay-Monk' was the greatest beneficiary of the campaign to avenge the death of shogun Yoshinori. His family's fortunes were restored and Sōzen went on to become one of the leaders in the Ōnin War.

Akamatsu Mitsusuke was perfectly satisfied that he had exacted a just revenge against the Bakufu, but as soon as shogun Yoshinori had been murdered Mitsusuke prepared himself for the inevitable act of suicide that he would have to perform when a punitive force was unleashed against his mansion. Yet hours went by and nothing happened, so Mitsusuke and his followers decamped for the safety of their castles in Harima Province, taking the shogun's severed head with them. The delay in revenge was puzzling at several levels, but according to a later investigation, 'There were none to disembowel themselves before the shogun and none to set out in pursuit'. Akamatsu Mitsusuke was therefore unlikely to have been alone in his scheming.[1]

It was not until a full three days after the assassination that the Bakufu decided that an expeditionary force should be mounted against the Akamatsu, but still no army marched west for another month. The Bakufu army that finally departed to seek justice was led by Hosokawa Shigeyuki (1434–1511), and leading the rearguard with his troops from Inaba and Hōki provinces was an ambitious leader who enters our story for the first time. He was called Yamana Mochitoyo and was a grandson of the man who had rebelled unsuccessfully against the shogun in 1391. Mochitoyo's branch of the Yamana

---

1 Varley, H. Paul, 1967, p. 69.

family had been allowed to continue in the Bakufu's service, and there was no one more enthusiastic about avenging shogun Yoshinori's death that Yamana Mochitoyo, who is known to history by two other appellations: his Buddhist title Yamana Sōzen and his nickname Aka Nyūdō or 'The Red Lay-Monk' from the scarlet colouration his countenance assumed in moments of anger.

When the avenging armies reached the Harima border Hosokawa Shigeyuki refused to allow the army to invade the province, a strange gesture which suggests that he too may have been in league with the Akamatsu. While he hesitated Yamana Sōzen took matters into his own hands and led the rearguard force into Harima Province. They attacked the Akamatsu stronghold on 9m 10d [25 September] and Mitsusuke killed himself, an act that *Akamatsu Monogatari* relates with great relish. He first forbade his young son from following him in death. The youth reluctantly made his escape, but on being apprehended committed suicide anyway. Meanwhile his father met his own end when he was told that the cause was lost:

> 'Then that settles the matter', replied Akamatsu, and turning to face eastwards he clasped his hands and invoked Amaterasu the Goddess of the Sun. He also prayed to Hachiman in the words 'Namu Hachiman Dai Bōsatsu', then turning round to face the west he prayed for rebirth and ended his sixty-one years of existence by committing *seppuku*. Sixty-nine of his followers joined him in death.[2]

Mitsusuke's death was followed by that of Akana Yukihide, the retainer of the Akamatsu who had delivered the actual sword thrust that had killed the shogun. In preparation for his heroic suicide Yukihide dressed calmly in a fine suit of armour patterned with tiny cherry blossoms. Suitably attired for the occasion, he shouted down a challenge to which a samurai called Murano Kageyasu responded. The latter is described as a strong man who used a bow that needed five men to string it. The arrow buried itself deep into the shaft of Yukihide's *naginata*. More arrows followed and sank firmly into the tower's superstructure, so Yukihide made a rapid descent to take on Kageyasu in single combat.

Other enemy horsemen met him as he arrived, but Yukihide was a 'matchless warrior' and took on his adversaries in the 'four-corners, eight sides' style of fighting, furiously felling thirteen men with his *naginata*. Murano Kageyasu appraised the situation and regretted that he could not settle the matter just by putting an arrow into the 'demon', so he leapt from his horse with a challenge to Yukihide. Yukihide heard the challenge and replied to it with a smile while taking hold of his own weapon with great skill and attacked his opponent 'with a dancing step'. Kageyasu responded

---

2   Yashiro, Kazuo 1994 *Akamatsu Monogatari: Kakitsu ki* (Tokyo, Bensei), pp.174–175.

in kind, and they fought each other, but because they were both very strong warriors, they struggled for a whole hour with no sign of a decision going one way or the other. Yukihide then used the butt of his *naginata* to strike his enemy on the front of his helmet. It must have stunned him because the impact settled Kageyasu's fate, and a thrust from Yukihide's weapon pierced his slender neck to kill him. Kageyasu was 27 years old. Yukihide then despatched himself.[3]

Akana Yukihide used this technique of ramming the butt of a *naginata* into his opponent's face when he went into action to follow his master Akamatsu Mitsusuke in death.

The castle was quickly destroyed by the victorious Yamana Sōzen, who had acted so rapidly that no other loyal *shugo*'s troops were there to assist him in his achievement. This precipitous move by Sōzen therefore ensured that the greatest beneficiary from the Kakitsu Incident was Yamana Sōzen himself. Akamatsu Mitsusuke's head was sent to Kyoto as proof of duty done and displayed for all to see, but the cautious Sōzen held back from staging a triumphant return to the capital. Instead, he plundered Harima, most of which he soon received as his reward from the Bakufu. The remaining districts of Harima would also be given to Yamana Sōzen in 1444. Governorships in the provinces of Mimasaka and Bizen were presented to other members of his family, so the ultimate outcome was that Sōzen's great

---

3   Yashiro, Kazuo 1994, pp.175–177.

act of loyalty to the Bakufu meant that by the time of the Ōnin War his family fortunes had been restored to the position they had occupied prior to his grandfather's unfortunate rebellion in 1391. By exacting revenge for the shogun's death another key player had moved forcibly on to the stage of the forthcoming Ōnin War.

The 1441 *tokusei ikki*

One additional reason why the punitive force had been so slow to set off following the Kakitsu Incident was that a new shogun was needed to ensure the stability of the Bakufu. This time there was no need to draw lots for a candidate because the choice of heir was obvious: Ashikaga Yoshikatsu (1433–1443), the eight-year-old son of Yoshinori, who became the seventh Ashikaga shogun. He was a course a minor, and to add to the chaos surrounding his father's murder, the year 1441 would see another *tokusei-ikki* or debt-cancelling riot. It will be recalled that the serious uprising of 1428 had taken place at the time of a shogun's accession, and 1441 provided another test for the popular belief that a change of regime was an ideal opportunity for the new ruler to display his 'virtuous rule' by cancelling debts.

The 1441 *tsuchi-ikki* would turn out to be the largest that took place at any time during the Muromachi Period and, in contrast to the apparent spontaneity of the uprising of 1428, the Kakitsu Ikki showed evidence of considerable planning. The timing was also very well chosen, because the *ikki* struck while the Bakufu's back was turned because of their expedition against the Akamatsu, which had required them to commit many troops to Harima Province and leave the capital vulnerable. The rioting began in Ōmi Province where local *ikki* members confronted the samurai of the provincial governor Kyōgoku Mochikiyo (1407–1470), and towards the end of the eighth lunar month more rioters began to gather on the outskirts of Kyoto. In mid-September there were clashes beside the temple of Kiyomizudera between *ikki* members and samurai from the Kyōgoku family. Ten rioters were killed against 53 of the supposedly superior samurai, which strongly suggests that members of the warrior class were to be found within the *ikki* ranks. There were separate incidents of arson and rioting elsewhere on the city outskirts, and on 20 September various groups converged on Kyoto from different directions, blocking roads and seizing strategic buildings. A priest from Tōji recorded that, 'every day they raid into the centre of the city'. The rioters threatened the Tōji priests that they would burn the temple down if the shogun did not issue a *tokusei*. By 22 September all seven entrances to Kyoto were in the hands of the rioters and the city's markets were empty of goods. The owners of private storehouses hired vigilantes to defend their property.

The *ikki* activity increased considerably when news reached Kyoto of the Akamatsu's defeat. No doubt expecting armies to return to the capital any day, the rioters racked up the pressure while they still had the chance. Within a week the Bakufu issued a debt cancellation edict that applied to

THE ŌNIN WAR

commoners only, but the *ikki* refused to accept it, insisting that the decree should apply to all classes of society. This sounds like a very selfless gesture, but it probably had more to do with getting on the right side of the military class when the armies returned to the capital. Three days later the Bakufu acquiesced to the additional clause. It was the first time in Japanese history that a government had bowed to the wishes of commoners, and these particular commoners moved quickly to see that the *tokusei* was honoured, attacking the pawnbrokers and forcing them to hand over any written records of indebtedness. The blockade of Kyoto was gradually lifted, but the wary *ikki* stayed in control of the city's lines of communication for one full month before withdrawing.

Ashikaga Yoshimasa

Ashikaga Yoshimasa (1435–1490) was the eighth Ashikaga shogun and will forever be associated with the Ōnin War. His appetite for luxury and extravagance was notorious, and his desire to abdicate led to a major split among his followers.

The child shogun Ashikaga Yoshikatsu's turbulent reign lasted for only one year before he died, supposedly by falling from a horse. He was succeeded by his younger brother Yoshimasa (1435–1490), another eight-year-old shogun who would eventually reign for 49 years and whose name would forever be indelibly associated with the Ōnin War. Yoshimasa was the eighth Ashikaga shogun, and his whole life would be dogged both by tragedy and heavy criticism of his luxurious tastes. The tragedies were real enough: his father had been murdered and his elder brother had been killed in an accident, but to add to these personal traumas the traditional view of the origins of the Ōnin War places the responsibility fully on the shoulders of Yoshimasa. Indeed, the first chapter of *Ōnin ki* has as its title 'Extravagance before the Conflict' and almost its first words are, 'The fault lay with shogun Yoshimasa'.[4]

Surveying the Muromachi Period from the lofty heights of the Tokugawa era the historian Arai Hakuseki stated that, 'For forty-nine years Yoshimasa's extravagance was unbridled, and both the daimyo and the common people were plunged into the depths of misery; the result was that the Ashikaga shogunate was finally destroyed'.[5] This is the image that has dogged Ashikaga Yoshimasa's memory for six centuries.

---

4   Shimura, Kunihiro. 2017. *Ōnin ki*. Tokyo, Chikuma Shobō, p.12.
5   Ackroyd, Joyce (Trans.). 1982, p.261.

FAMINE, FAMILY AND FAVOURITISM

In fairness to him, he tried to control the power of the *shugo* while he was still a young man, but the murder of his father had damaged the Ashikaga shogun's authority forever, so as the years went by Yoshimasa slipped further and further into an abandonment of harsh reality while the contrast between the shogun's court life and the misery of his subjects grew even wider.

As part of its condemnation of Ashikaga Yoshimasa, *Ōnin ki* makes a brief but specific reference to the suffering of the people to provide a contrast to the extravagance of the upper classes. No further details are provided as to the actual nature of the pains endured by the commoners, so we have to look elsewhere to understand the enormity of the natural disasters and their human consequences that struck Japan between 1457 and 1461: the *nengo* of Chōroku and Kanshō. Drastic climate fluctuations seem to have occurred throughout this time and eclipsed the effects of the famines that had prompted the 1428 and 1441 uprisings. In 1459 there was a particularly severe drought, followed later in the same year by a typhoon that hit Kyoto, wrecking many dwellings and sweeping thousands of their inhabitants into the flooded Kamo River. Unsen Taikyoku of the Kōfukuji recorded in *Hekizan Nichiroku* what he witnessed for himself when he looked down on the scene from the Shijō Bridge:

> I saw countless numbers of bodies heaped up as if they had been just roofing tiles or stones. There were so many of them that they had interrupted the flow of the river, and the stench that arose is beyond all understanding. I then walked across the city from east to west, all the while trying to control my tears and to toughen myself up against these scenes. It is said that from the first month of this year until now there have been 82,000 deaths in the capital. How do I know this? There is a certain monk who lives in northern Kyoto. He made 82,000 little wooden sotōba, one of which he placed on every corpse he came across. It is said that he now has only 2,000 sotōba left, and it should be noted that there are still many more bodies lying within the capital and outside in the fields that have not been marked in this way.[6]

The tragedy would later be recorded by Kikei Shinzui in his *Inryōken nichiroku* with the words, 'The stench of the corpses in Rakuchū has now died away. How refreshing that is', but the terrible years were still not over.[7] A swarm of locusts devastated what few crops appeared in 1460, and in the famine areas of Bizen and Mimasaka Provinces there were reports

---

6   Quoted in Ishinomori, Shōtarō. 2017b. *Ōhō-fubō no hametsu – Ōnin no Ran*. Tokyo: Chūokoronsha, p.46.
7   Quoted in Various Authors. 2006. *Hosokawa Katsumoto - Yamana Sōzen to Ōnin no Ran. (Nihon no kassen Series, 48)*. (Tokyo: Kodansha), p.12.

of cannibalism. Drought returned in 1461, driving thousands more starving people into Kyoto so that the streets became full of destitute and dying people. The temples that provided relief were overwhelmed by the unprecedented scale of the demands placed upon them.

To add to the misery the hordes of starving people in Kyoto were joined by rioters from the countryside demanding a fresh round of *tokusei*. *Ikki* from Kawachi headed for Kyoto and occupied Tōji during the tenth month, from where they attacked the usual targets of brewers, pawnbrokers and food storage facilities. Just as had happened in 1441, the moneylenders paid samurai to fight off the *ikki*, but the latter drove away the mercenaries and then took on a force of 800 men sent by the Bakufu whom they also dispersed. In a further skirmish on 11m 9d [3 December] the Bakufu forces killed the *ikki*'s ringleaders. During a different incursion into the capital in 1462 two entire city blocks of Kyoto were burned out, and by the time of further riots in 1465 it had become clear that erstwhile vassals of the Bakufu had joined the mobs. A decree was therefore issued threatening the confiscation of property from anyone found to be involved. The command cannot have worked, because it was followed by a stricter decree ordering any vassals who might even be 'obstinately sympathising with them' to remove themselves to the city and stay there until the disturbances had ended.[8]

In the midst of all this mayhem, shogun Ashikaga Yoshimasa stayed intent upon his pleasures, one of which was the construction of fine palaces. Only in his building projects was Yoshimasa ever assertive; otherwise, he took little interest in political events and was easily swayed, changing his mind and his direction of support on numerous occasions. In 1462 Yoshimasa built the luxurious Takakura Palace for his mother at a time when all around him were suffering. His callous conduct was so scandalous that it even drew a poetic rebuke from Emperor Go-Hanazono, who 'took no joy in verse while the suffering people struggled to gather ferns to eat'.[9] Yoshimasa was sufficiently chastened by the rebuke that he suspended the building programme for a while, only to resume it later for the lavish interior decoration of his mother's mansion. It was only after further extreme pressure that he exercised several rounds of *tokusei* for the cancelling of debts, although even this had a cynical side. As Arai Hakuseki wrote, 'he decreed a *Tokusei*, a measure unheard of in the previous age, and during his rule he has decreed them thirteen times so that the coffers of the pawn-brokers and people's private purses are completely exhausted'.[10] When *tokusei* edicts rendered the pledges void it caused a backlash by

---

8 Davis, David L. 1974 'Ikki in Late Medieval Japan' in Hall, John W. & Mass, Jeffrey P. *Medieval Japan: Essays in Institutional History.* Stanford: Stanford University Press, p.230.
9 Varley, H. Paul. 1967, p.118.
10 Ackroyd, Joyce (Trans.). 1982, p.260.

The Kinkakuji or Golden Pavilion, the vibrant symbol of the reign of the third Ashikaga shogun Yoshimitsu, who is remembered for his wise and successful rule.

The shogun's palace in Kyoto was known as the Palace of Flowers. It survived the Ōnin War until 1476.

THE ŌNIN WAR

Hosokawa Katsumoto (1430-73) was the leader of the Eastern Army during the Ōnin War. Katsumoto was a gifted administrator, and before the war he enjoyed two terms of office as Kyoto Kanrei (shogun's deputy). Katsumoto became Kanrei again in 1468 and stayed in office until his death in 1473. Throughout the entire conflict he controlled both the emperor and the ex-emperor and had made them declare the Western Army to be rebels against the throne.

Yamana Sōzen Mochitoyo (1404-73), the 'Red Lay Monk', led the Western Army. His nickname (Aka Nyūdō) came from the scarlet colouration his countenance assumed in moments of anger. He was a grandson of the man who had rebelled unsuccessfully against the shogun in 1391, but restored his family to favour when he avenged the murder of shogun Yoshinori. The opportunistic victory gained by Sōzen alone ensured that the greatest beneficiary from the horrific incident was Yamana Sōzen himself. Yamana Sōzen's Kyoto mansion was surprisingly close to that of his enemy, being only one block over and one down from Katsumoto's home, and when war broke out between them much damage was caused in that area of Kyoto.

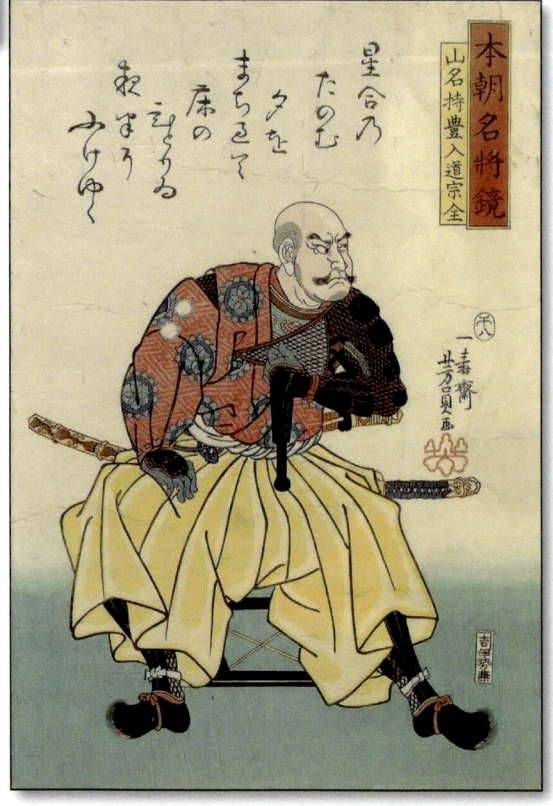

Ashikaga Yoshimasa, the much-maligned shogun whose behaviour led to the outbreak of the Ōnin War but who went on to lead a cultural revival.

A contemporary street scene with architecture typical of the districts of Kyoto where the fighting of the Ōnin War took place. This model is in Osaka City Museum.

THE ŌNIN WAR

A section from the *Shinnyodō emaki* of 1524, showing a battle of the Ōnin War.

This section from the *Kiyomizudera engi emaki* of 1520 shows typical arms and armour of the time of the Ōnin War. The predominant samurai weapons are bows and *naginata*. The scroll tells the story of a battle against demons, so their weapons are of an imaginary design compared to the authentic samurai weapons.

Street fighting, from a painted screen, showing samurai engaging outside a gateway. The scene depicted is from Japan's twelfth-century Gempei War, but the weapons and tactics were not much different during the fifteenth century. The big changes that came with the Ōnin War were the widespread use of arson and the depredations of the gangs of ashigaru whom the leaders let run riot.

Another section from the *Kiyomizudera engi emaki* showing samurai in battle. One of the fleeing demons holds an authentic *nagamaki*, a weapon that is a cross between a long sword and a pole arm.

THE ŌNIN WAR

The main hall of the temple of Shōkokuji, which was rebuilt early in the seventeenth century after being burned down during the Ōnin War.

The depredations of ashigaru are perfectly captured in this section from the *Shinnyodō emaki* of 1524. Instead of engaging in warfare they are destroying a building and looting its contents.

The Ginkaku or Silver Pavilion is the sombre symbol of the age which followed the Ōnin War and saw a cultural revival that was characterised by restraint.

An armour of *dō-maru* style, typical of the Ōnin War period: © Tokyo National Museum

THE ŌNIN WAR

The Yasaka pagoda, one of only two buildings in the heart of Kyoto to have survived the terrible Ōnin War. The five-storey story tall pagoda was a 15th-century addition to a 6th-century temple complex known as Hōkan-ji. The other building to have survived is Daihōonji, popularly known as Senbon Shakadō, which is illustrated within the text.

The spirit of the terrible Ōnin War is perfectly captured in this picture, which shows a samurai on foot wielding a long, heavy wood and iron club against a poorly armed but fierce ashigaru in a hand-to-hand combat within Japan's capital of Kyoto. In the background a shrine burns, evidence of the arson attacks that were a persistent feature of the bitter street fighting that took place. Illustration by Giorgio Albertini © Helion & Company 2021

cutting the normal taxes paid to the Bakufu, but the wily Yoshimasa also saw the issuing of *tokusei* as a way of raising funds for his lavish palaces.

History has blackened Yoshimasa's name for the above, but there are several anecdotes depicting him being moved by what he heard of the peoples' tribulations, and it is recorded that in 1459 he presented some token gifts to relieve the suffering arising from the current famine. Yoshimasa is supposed to have been inclined in that direction through having been warned in a dream by the ghost of his father, who ordered Yoshimasa to give alms in order to relieve Yoshinori of the pains he was suffering in Hell. Yoshimasa is also believed to have supported the priest Ganami in the latter's celebrated relief efforts, whereby temporary housing was built, and the people were fed on chestnut and rice porridge, paid for by donations. Nevertheless, Yoshimasa continued to indulge in flower viewing parties while the famine was at its height. *Ōnin ki* provides an example:

> A 'feast of one thousand delicacies' was prepared for the flower-viewing party. The shogun's own attendants had chopsticks of gold, while the other guests had chopsticks made from perfumed wood covered in gold leaf. People went quite mad in their efforts to acquire their costumes, which were so expensive that they were forced either to pawn or sell their belongings.[11]

Ashikaga Yoshimi (1439-1491) was the half-brother of Yoshimasa who reluctantly accepted the shogun's request for him to be declared heir.

It was not long before Yoshimasa realised that beautiful buildings and lavish parties could only ever provide a ruler with the outward sign of genuine power, and when he appreciated that no amount of effort on his part was going to restore the Bakufu to the former glory it had enjoyed he gave up trying and sought solace in dissipation and pleasure. Surrounded by toadies he was shielded from blame, immune from criticism and increasingly oblivious to the suffering elsewhere. Yet Yoshimasa was still shogun and had the responsibility of ruling Japan, so if he wanted to separate himself completely from the real world there was only one course of action left, and that was to abdicate in favour of an heir.

---

11   Shimura, Kunihiro. 2017, p.14.

THE ŌNIN WAR

As the pages above have shown, this was by no means an uncommon practice, but Yoshimasa had no son. His wife Hino Tomiko had failed to produce an heir, so Yoshimasa persuaded his younger half-brother Ashikaga Yoshimi (1439–1491) to re-enter the secular life from the priesthood and become his successor. Yoshimi was very reluctant to comply, fearing for his fate if Yoshimasa did succeed in producing a son of his own, but Yoshimasa assured him that even if a child was born, he would not go back on his promise to Yoshimi. The latter was satisfied with the pledge and re-entered the laity in 1464 as the adopted son of the shogun. The way was now open for Yoshimasa to achieve his desire of happy retirement, but the following year Hino Tomiko finally gave birth to a son: the future shogun Yoshihisa. *Ōnin ki* sums up what this would mean for Japan. 'She brooded over how she could get her own son established as the heir. She had bitter thoughts towards Yoshimi, whom she despised, and hoped that a miracle might occur that would change the situation. It was this desire by Lady Tomiko that her son should succeed that eventually led to war.'[12]

Hino Tomiko was the wife of shogun Yoshimasa. When she gave birth to a son – the future shogun Yoshihisa – Yoshimi's succession was placed in doubt, and their resulting rivalry helped give rise to the Ōnin War.

Yet more than desire was needed for war. There had to be armed support, and that would be supplied by two crucial individuals. The first was Hosokawa Katsumoto, who was a member of one of the three *shugo* families who alternated among themselves the post of Kyoto Kanrei - the shogun's deputy in the capital. Hosokawa Katsumoto was a gifted administrator and by the time of the Ōnin War he had enjoyed two terms of office as Kanrei.

---

12   Shimura, Kunihiro. 2017, p.19.

Katsumoto became Kanrei again in 1468 and stayed in office until his death in 1473. The other was Yamana Sōzen, who was Katsumoto's father-in-law. He inherited the reins of the family in 1432 and in 1440 he became head of the *samurai-dokoro*. As noted earlier he led the main punitive force after the Kakitsu Incident, defeating Mitsusuke and gaining the Akamatsu's domains, including Harima, to become *shugo* of eight provinces. In 1450 he became a Buddhist monk.

The Hatakeyama Succession Dispute

Battered on one side by natural disasters and on another by political rivalries, the increasingly detached Ashikaga Yoshimasa also had to cope with an ominous succession dispute within the influential Hatakeyama family. Their rivalry would prove to be of such long duration that it kickstarted the Ōnin War and then outlasted the conflict for another half century. The background to the dispute is as follows. In 1442 it became the Hatakeyama's turn to fill the post of shogun's deputy in the capital, and the succession had gone to Hatakeyama Mochikuni (1397–1455). At that time shogun Yoshimasa was only eight years old so the deputy's influence was considerable. Mochikuni died in 1455, by which time a succession dispute had long been brewing because he had failed to produce a male heir. Mochikuni had consequently adopted his nephew Masanaga (1442–1493) and named him as his future successor but, as a strange harbinger of the shogun's future problems, shortly afterwards one of Mochikuni's concubines gave birth to a boy: Hatakeyama Yoshinari (1437–1491). The traditional account of the affair states that Mochikuni doted on the new arrival and would not rest until he had installed Yoshinari as his rightful heir, which he did formally on retiring in 1450 in blatant disregard of the promise he had previously made to Masanaga.

Hatakeyama Yoshinari (1437-1491) was the rival of his cousin and adopted brother Masanaga (1442-1493). Their long and savage succession dispute kickstarted the Ōnin War and was still being fought over by their sons as late as 1499.

The new arrangements were approved of by shogun Yoshimasa in 1454, but the dispossessed Hatakeyama Masanaga had powerful allies who were willing to support his cause, and among them were the two powerful *shugo* Yamana Sōzen and Hosokawa Katsumoto. At this stage they were acting in concert, and their pressure helped the young shogun to change his mind in favour of Masanaga. Fighting between the Hatakeyama began during the famine years of Chōroku and Kanshō in precisely the same areas where the *ikki* had operated and where the famine had been suffered the most. Highly alarmed, the shogun performed a further U-turn and changed back to supporting Yoshinari. Fearing retribution, Hatakeyama Masanaga fled to his castle in Kawachi Province. The shogun tried peace talks, but Hosokawa Katsumoto pressed Masanaga's case so successfully in the shogun's presence that Masanaga was allowed to return to Kyoto in 1459. Unfortunately, the immediate result of the shogun's conciliatory gestures was that the fighting which had been confined to the mountains became replicated at a close distance to Kyoto where, of course, huge disruption was already being caused by natural disasters and *ikki* incursions. Yoshimasa's reaction was to transfer his allegiance back to Masanaga once again and banish Yoshinari from the capital in 1460.

Hatakeyama Yoshinari, who was probably now as confused as he was scared, sought refuge in Wakae Castle in Kawachi Province, the headquarters of his fervent supporter Yusa Kunisuke. Hatakeyama Masanaga then received an official commission from the shogun to destroy his rival. He set off with a small force and set up camp at Tatsuta in Yamato Province, where he received information that a surprise attack was about to be launched against him from Wakae. At dawn the following morning Yusa Kunisuke led the planned raid on Masanaga's army and achieved a measure of surprise, but the results were not what he had planned. Instead of gaining a rapid victory his men were confused by the unfamiliar terrain and driven off. Their leader Yusa Kunisuke was one of the victims, so when the news of the failure reached Hatakeyama Yoshinari in Wakae he abandoned his position and headed for the greater security of a fortress on top of Takeyama.

Hatakeyama Masanaga's confident troops swept on into Kawachi and set up lines around Takeyama, but the castle was not to be easily taken and a long siege developed that was to last throughout the winter of 1460 and into the spring of 1461. Even a daring night raid by the defenders under the protection of a smoke screen during the sixth month of 1461 failed to dislodge Masanaga's besiegers, and when the siege dragged on into a second winter the shogun sent reinforcements to aid the stubborn Masanaga. Among their leaders was Yamana Koretoyo, the son of Sōzen, leading troops from Bingo Province. 'He led seven attacks and was repulsed seven times, but the final assault left the garrison exhausted, forcing Yoshinari himself to emerge sword in hand at the head of his army to repel the attackers. As the sun went down Koretoyo withdrew to the lines'.[13]

The key to Yoshinari's long-lasting and successful defence of Takeyama lay in his control of the supply route to Kii Province. It seems to have taken his rival Masanaga a long time to appreciate that fact, but in 1463 he managed to cut the road and establish secure control of Takeyama's communications.

---

13 Shimura, Kunihiro. 2017, p.34.

FAMINE, FAMILY AND FAVOURITISM

Finally, after nearly three years on the mountain, Yoshinari abandoned his position and fled. He passed through a series of refuges including Kōyasan until arriving ultimately in Yoshino, and the news of his defeat was greeted with much rejoicing in Kyoto. Masanaga was summoned back to the capital by a grateful shogun and returned in triumph in 1463. By then it looked as though Yoshinari's star had fallen forever, but once Hosokawa Katsumoto and Yamana Sōzen started choosing opposing sides in whatever dispute came along, Yoshinari discovered that he had an ally in the latter simply because Hosokawa Katsumoto had long been Masanaga's supporter:

> At this point, Yamana Nyūdō Sōzen, having witnessed Yoshinari's prowess at the Takeyama fort some years before, and thinking that it would be advantageous to his own house if he brought him over to his side, prevailed on his elder sister the nun Ansein to importune Tomiko daily on his behalf, with the result that Yoshinari was presently restored to favour. He went to Kyoto and presented himself at Yoshimasa's palace on the twenty-fifth day of the twelfth month of the first year of Bunshō.[14]

In the final month of 1466 Hatakeyama Yoshinari rode through Kyoto at the head of an army to set up a base at the Senbon Shakadō.[15] Ironically, this temple was to become the only building in Northern Kyoto to survive the Ōnin War. The two Hatakeyama rivals were now back in the capital and were ready to start fighting each other all over again.

Daihōonji, popularly known as Senbon Shakadō, is the only temple to have survived within the area of northern Kyoto that saw the bulk of the fighting during the Ōnin War. In 1466 Hatakeyama Yoshinari made it his base when he entered Kyoto.

---

14 Ackroyd, Joyce (Trans.). 1982, p.253.
15 Goza, Yūichi. 2016. *Ōnin no Ran Sengoku jidai o undo tairan*. Tokyo: Chūō Kōronsha, p.82.

5

The Battle of the Kami Goryō Shrine

The Kami Goryō Shrine lies just to the north of the Shōkokuji temple complex in northern Kyoto. It is a peaceful little green oasis nowadays because the shrine's courtyard contains the last vestiges of the forest that enclosed it in the year 1467 when the Hatakeyama rivals fought a fierce battle around and within its site. The fighting took place between the 17th and 18th days of the first lunar month [21–22 February] of what would shortly be named as the First Year of Ōnin. The site's great historical significance is commemorated by a simple stone monument which states that the battle at the Kami Goryō Shrine was the first conflict of the Ōnin War. Technically this is not quite true, because the Ōnin *nengō* was declared retrospectively on the fifth day of

The Kami Goryō Shrine was the location of the first battle of the Ōnin War, but the skirmish was followed by a few months of peace.

THE BATTLE OF THE KAMI GORYŌ SHRINE

the third lunar month [9 April] and the action at Kami Goryō was followed by several months of peace. Nevertheless, even if the battle of Kami Goryō launched what was in some sense a 'phoney war', the encounter is highly significant in that it was fought within Kyoto as a curtain raiser for what would soon follow.

The background to the skirmish at Kami Goryō was the long-lasting dispute between the two members of the Hatakeyama clan who had already been at war with each other for ten years and in and out of favour with the shogun for much longer than that. As Arai Hakuseki (drawing on *Ōnin ki*) put it two centuries later, 'the two branches of Hatakeyama together, during an interval of barely twenty-four years… suffered confiscation of their estate three times and were pardoned three times'.[1] We noted above that Hatakeyama Yoshinari had once again regained his position in Kyoto society. Now rehabilitated he pressed on with the long-lasting rivalry, but the scenario was Kyoto itself, not some distant mountain in Kawachi, and the New Year festivities provided a testbed for other parties' loyalties. Fearful of upsetting Yamana Sōzen, the shogun cancelled his traditional visit to the mansion of his deputy which would normally occur on the second day of the first month. The deputy was Hatakeyama Masanaga, and shortly afterwards he dismissed Masanaga from his post, ordering him to hand over certain lands to Yoshinari.

Buoyed up with confidence by this gesture of approval, Yamana Sōzen urged Hosokawa Katsumoto to follow the shogun's example and abandon his support for Masanaga, and when he refused Sōzen asked the shogun's permission to punish Katsumoto for his insubordination. Yoshimasa's sole response was to issue a mild rebuke to Katsumoto, so that same evening Sōzen moved the shogun's chosen heir Ashikaga Yoshimi to the safety of the Bakufu headquarters. Hosokawa Katsumoto's reaction to the gesture was to summon troops to his own mansion and make defensive preparations.[2] Thoroughly alarmed, Yoshimasa ordered Yamana and Hosokawa to stay out of the Hatakeyama dispute and added that the first to defy the order would be declared a rebel by imperial decree, a command which neither dared refuse. Hatakeyama Masanaga then held a council of war, and *Ōnin ki* puts the following words into the mouth of his follower Jinbō Naganobu:

> Katsumoto has agreed to the shogun's demands that he provides no further assistance to us, but our enemy is based in the Bakufu headquarters and will certainly use whatever secret information he has to our detriment. This mansion of ours is built on an area of flatland that allows us no strategic advantage, so to face a battle here could be disastrous. It is always said that one should either advance or retreat depending upon the prevailing situation, so if we abandon

---

1 Ackroyd, Joyce (Trans.). 1982, p.259
2 Goza, Yūichi. 2016, p.82.

THE ŌNIN WAR

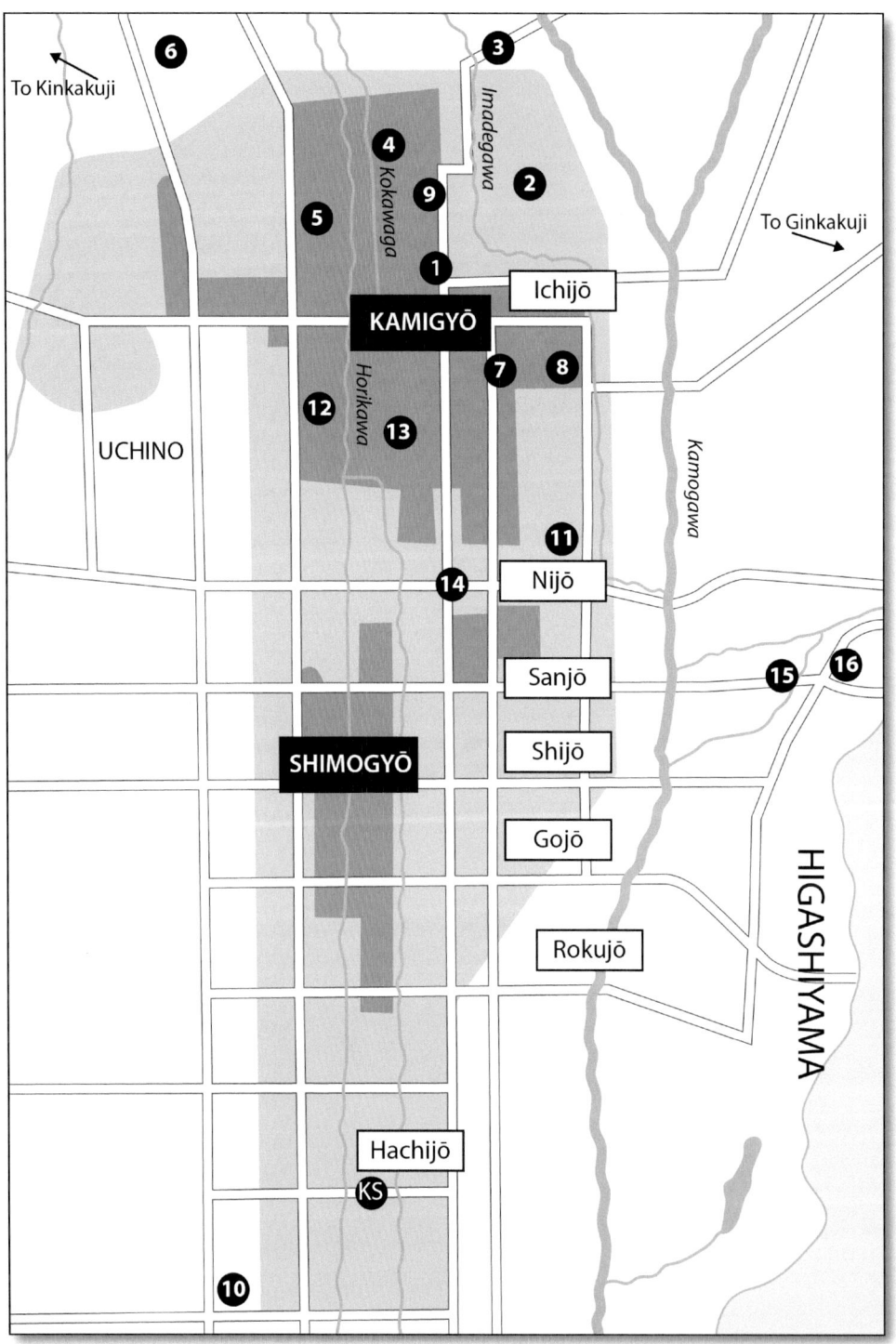

Kyoto during the Ōnin War. The outer grey area shows the approximate limits of the city at the time; the darker shading shows the areas worst affected by fires and destruction. Kamigyō is the upper aristocratic quarter, Shimogyō the realm of the townspeople. To help with the reader's orientation, 'KS' indicates the location of present-day Kyoto Station. Key: 1. The Palace of Flowers; 2. Shōkokuji; 3. Kami Goryō Shrine; 4. Hosokawa Katsumoto's mansion; 5. Yamana Sōzen's mansion; 6. Funaokayama; 7. Imperial Palace; 8. Sanbō-In; 9. Isshiki Yoshinao's mansion; 10. Tōji; 11. Hatakeyama Masanaga's mansion; 12. Isshiki Gorō's mansion; 13 Shiba Yoshikado's mansion; 14. Tōjiji; 15. Shōren-In; 16. Nanzenji.

THE BATTLE OF THE KAMI GORYŌ SHRINE

this place and move to the Kami Goryō Shrine we should be able to hold our ground by making use of the forest cover for defensive purposes. If we become really hard-pressed then Katsumoto must surely be forced to abandon his neutrality and come to our aid.[3]

Naganobu finished his speech by suggesting that if everything seemed hopeless, they could even attack the imperial palace.

Hatakeyama Masanaga agreed with Naganobu's advice. As the accompanying map makes clear, his mansion was perilously isolated from the Hosokawa strongpoints in northern Kyoto, so he abandoned it for what he believed was the greater security of the Kami Goryō Shrine. Masanaga knew that his home would be destroyed as soon as it was vacant, so his final act was to burn it down himself. He entered the Kami Goryō Shrine on 1m 17d [21 February 1467] and at dawn on the eighteenth day Yoshinari attacked the place. It was the first military action other than *ikki* activity seen within Kyoto itself since the Ōei Rebellion of 1399.

Hatakeyama Yoshinari's ally Yamana Sōzen had already taken precautions in case the day went against his friend and ally. Suspecting that an attack on the imperial palace could be a real possibility, Sōzen was instrumental in persuading the shogun that the emperor and his family should be moved to the safety of the Bakufu headquarters. That having been done, his comrade Hatakeyama Yoshinari felt that his rear was secure and that victory had been handed to him on a plate, so he advanced confidently against Masanaga's position in the Kami Goryō Shrine. *Ōnin ki* describes how the action began:

> Yoshinari's ally Yusa Kawachi-no-Kami jumped down from his horse and hurried to be at the forefront of the attack. Other warriors quickly joined him, abandoning their horses so as to be able to engage with the enemy. They began by setting fire to the village of Shōmonji that lay beside the *torii* gate of the shrine, but just at that point a storm blew down from Mount Atago. The swirling snow mingled with the flames and blew into the eyes and mouths of the attacking force, confusing them so much that they ran around with no sense of direction. The defenders realised the predicament that Yoshinari's men now found themselves in so, after waiting for the right moment under the direction of the famous Takeda Yoji, they unleashed volley after volley of arrows and cut them down. All the generals in Yoshinari's vanguard were felled... Six hundred men from Yusa's force alone were wounded. Neither shield nor armour could withstand the arrows loosed out of the thicket.[4]

---

3   Shimura, Kunihiro. 2017, pp.45–46.
4   Shimura, Kunihiro. 2017, p.48.

THE ŌNIN WAR

Ōnin ki continues with an anecdote typical of its style of narrative about the death of a young samurai with blackened teeth in the fashion of a courtier and dressed in a splendid suit of armour. He issues a challenge but is immediately felled by an arrow from the defending archers.[5] It was a portent of more tragedy to follow. Yoshinari's harassed attackers were soon joined by reinforcements under Asakura Takakage (1428–1481) but still Masanaga's determined defence held firm from within the forest. More reinforcements for the besiegers appeared under Yamana Masatoyo (1441–1499), another son of Yamana Sōzen and living proof that the latter's promised neutrality had been secretly discarded. The tide of battle soon began to go their way, but it was already growing dark so both sides withdrew to their respective lines. That night, according to *Ōnin ki*, the desperate Jinbō Naganobu sent a pathetic message to one of his supporters outside. 'We are tired out from the battle of the day. There is nothing we can do about it because the shogun has ordered everyone not to help us. That is how it is, so please send me a barrel of *sake*. I will present it to Masanaga for his farewell banquet. Then we will both commit *seppuku*.'[6]

The news of Masanaga's impending defeat placed Hosokawa Katsumoto in a great dilemma. He was constrained from helping the beleaguered Masanaga because of the shogun's orders, but he was also fully aware that there was little he could do anyway to save his ally. Their confident enemies in the Yoshinari faction clearly had the ear of the shogun and also held the persons of the imperial family as hostages. The author of *Ōnin ki* would condemn Hosokawa Katsumoto for failing to come to the aid of his friend but notes that many people approved of his obedience to the shogun's wishes.

According to *Ōnin ki*, Masanaga's only chance was to make his enemies think that they had the upper hand and then escape to rally his supporters at some future date. Katsumoto conveyed these thoughts to Masanaga by means of a humming-bulb signalling arrow. Masanaga and his troops gathered

The Kami Goryō Shrine was razed to the ground during the fighting, and soon much of northern Kyoto would resemble this burned-out shrine building in Akita which was destroyed as the result of an accidental fire in 2006.

---

5   Shimura, Kunihiro. 2017 pp.48–49.
6   Shimura, Kunihiro. 2017, p.50.

THE BATTLE OF THE KAMI GORYŌ SHRINE

the bodies of those killed during the defence of Kami Goryō and made a funeral pyre out of the shrine buildings. The flames were too strong to allow Yoshinari's attackers anywhere near, so the survivors made their escape uninterrupted, crawling through the undergrowth as the bonfire blazed. By the time Yoshinari managed to search the embers Hatakeyama Masanaga was nowhere to be found. Had his rival perished, or merely escaped? With that question remaining unanswered for the time being, the battle of the Kami Goryō Shrine came to an end.

As noted earlier, the fight is conventionally regarded as the opening encounter of the Ōnin War, but even *Ōnin ki* states that, rather than marking a collapse into chaos, the Kami Goryō encounter was followed by several months of peace that settled upon the capital because, 'Yamana Sōzen and Hatakeyama Yoshinari were completely unaware that Masanaga had escaped. As the country returned to a state of rest, they were filled with happiness'.[7] So calm did things become that they ordered their soldiers to stand down and return to their home provinces, which the men did with great relief, 'shouting "Banzai" and singing songs of peace'.[8] But as the ashes cooled in the Kami Goryō Shrine the era name was changed and the First Year of Ōnin officially began.

---

7   Shimura, Kunihiro. 2017, p.54.
8   Shimura, Kunihiro. 2017, p.54.

6

The First Year of Ōnin

There was the occasional skirmish in Kyoto after the battle of Kami Goryō while Yamana Sōzen and Hatakeyama Yoshinari, 'who were enjoying life's luxuries to the utmost', celebrated their victory.[1] Otherwise the phoney war continued unabated until the fifth lunar month of the First Year of Ōnin, but long before any arrow was loosed in anger a considerable amount of political activity had taken place behind the scenes. Early in the third lunar month, while peace reigned and the Yamana were still the faction enjoying the shogun's favour, ominous rumours had begun spreading that a retainer of the Yamana had been murdered by a retainer of the Hosokawa. During that same third month Hosokawa Katsumoto was conspicuously absent from the shogun's court, and many suspected that he was planning a major move.

At precisely that point in the developments Hatakeyama Masanaga made a reappearance in Kyoto to swell the numbers of Katsumoto's supporters. There was also unrest in neighbouring provinces and a general move towards the capital as troops began arriving at the behest of both factions. *Ōnin ki* relates that on 5m 10d [11 June] Katsumoto's supporter Akamatsu Masanori invaded the territories of Harima and Bizen that had been given to Yamana Sōzen following

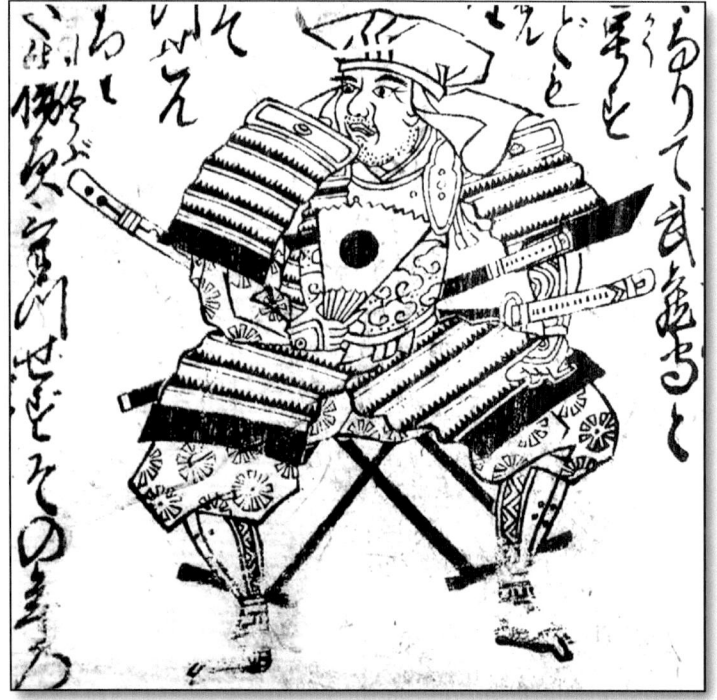

Hosokawa Katsumoto (1430–1473) was the leader of the so-called Eastern Army during the Ōnin War.

---

1 Shimura, Kunihiro. 2017, p.56.

THE FIRST YEAR OF ŌNIN

the disgrace of the Akamatsu in 1441. He also tried to enter Mimasaka Province but, on meeting resistance, he withdrew his forces and headed for Kyoto, where they would soon be sorely needed. Of the Hosokawa's other allies Shiba Yoshitoshi attacked rivals of his own in Owari and Tōtōmi while Takeda Nobukata assaulted the Isshiki in Wakasa; both then headed for Kyoto. Lesser-known names in Ise and Iga Provinces also grabbed the opportunity to settle a few old scores before moving to the capital to join either Hosokawa Katsumoto or Yamana Sōzen.[2] In *Gohōkōin ki* the monk diarist Konoe Masaie (1445–1505) provides figures for one particular move, noting that Ikeda Mitsumasa, a retainer of Hosokawa Matsumoto, left Settsu Province for Kyoto on 5m 16d [17 June] with 'twelve horsemen and 1,000 common soldiers'. On 20d [21 June] Konoe notes that Yamana Sōzen, Hatakeyama Yoshinari and Isshiki Yoshinao had joined forces at the mansion of Shiba Yoshikado.[3] To his fellow diarists Jinson and Kyōkaku it was the beginning of a frightening period of time; and the former lamented that, 'To East, West, South and North, there is no peace in the land.'[4]

The northern edge of the site of Hosokawa Katsumoto's mansion is marked today by this small, paved area adjacent to the temple of Hōkyōji. We are looking along the line of the former river called Kokawa from the site of the bridge of Dodobashi.

---

2   Shimura, Kunihiro. 2017, pp.59–60.
3   Goza, Yūichi. 2016, p.88.
4   Goza, Yūichi. 2016, pp.88–89.

THE ŌNIN WAR

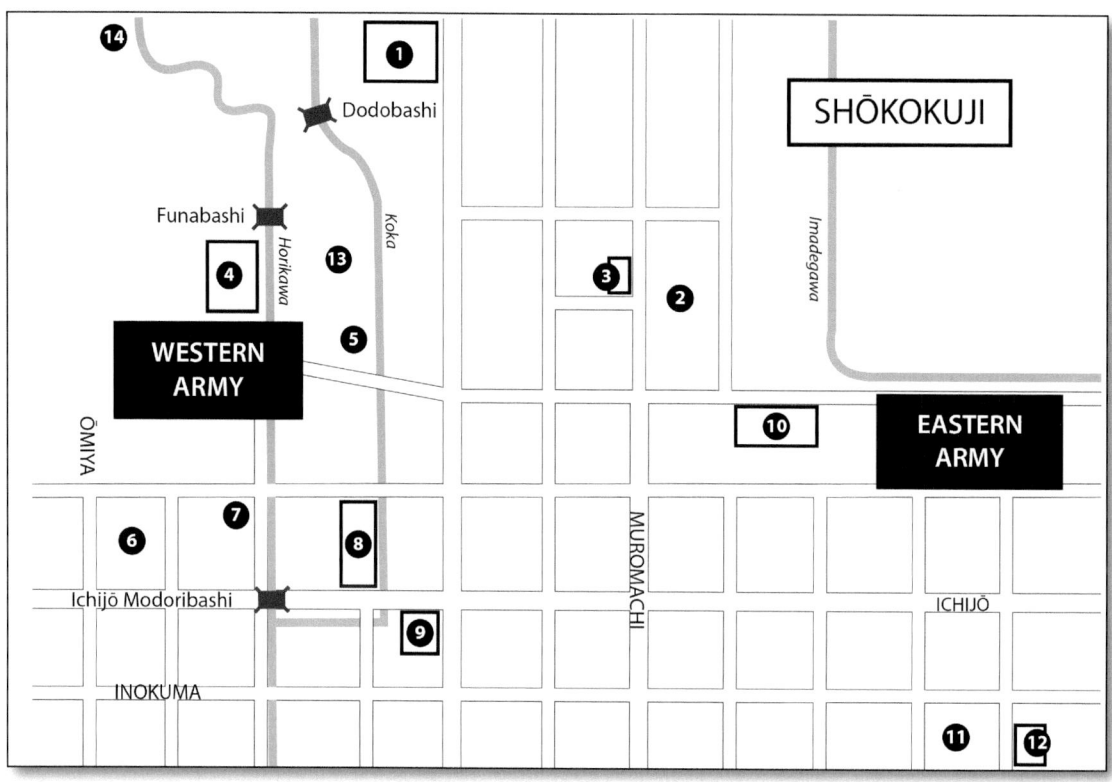

Northern Kyoto during the fighting of 1467. Key: 1. Hosokawa Katsumoto's mansion; 2. The Palace of Flowers; 3. Isshiki Yoshinao's mansion; 4. Yamana Sōzen's mansion; 5. Jissō-In; 6. Hosokawa Katsuhisa's mansion; 7. Kumonodera; 8. The temples of Hyakumanben, Kōdō and Gyōganji; 9. Hosokawa Shigeyuki's mansion; 10. Ashikaga Yoshimi's mansion; 11. Imperial Palace; 12. Sanbō-In; 13. Shōjitsubō; 14. Rozanji.

Kyoto's phoney war ended on 5m 26d [27 June] when Katsumoto's men attacked the mansion of Isshiki Yoshinao, one of Sōzen's leading generals. *Ōnin ki* explains this decisive move not as an assault on a randomly selected target but the result of strategic deliberations within the Hosokawa faction, and to understand the military considerations that must have exercised minds on both sides the reader's attention is drawn to Kyoto's historic grid layout of streets and how its communications were affected by a number of rivers. The shogun's Palace of Flowers lay between the avenues called Karasuma and Muromachi two blocks north of Ichijō, and immediately to the east of the palace was the temple of Shōkokuji. A river called Imadegawa flowed in a southerly direction through the grounds of Shōkokuji and then turned east and south to provide an outer line for the eastern extremity of the northern street grid. Another river, the Kokawa, also flowed southwards four blocks further over to the West and was crossed by the bridge called Dodobashi next to the mansion of Hosokawa Katsumoto. The Kokawa then flowed westwards along Ichijō to join the important river called the Horikawa. Nowadays much of the Horikawa is culverted, but some of it can still be seen and enjoyed along a tree-lined footpath beside the busy modern thoroughfare of Horikawa-dōri. This river was destined to act as no-man's land between the two warring sides, because Yamana Sōzen's mansion lay on its other side. It was surprisingly close to that of his enemy, being only one block over and one down from Katsumoto's home.

The temple of Shōkokuji was founded by Ashikaga Yoshimitsu and lay adjacent to the Palace of Flowers. It experienced much fierce fighting during the Ōnin War.

Based solely on the relative location of these two mansions, the rivals' spheres of influence fitted neatly into the appellation they would henceforth enjoy: the Eastern and Western Armies. 'East' and 'West', of course, bore no relation to what is now understood as eastern and western Kyoto; nor did it reflect the ancient division of Heian-kyō across Senbon Avenue. Their military bases were the mansions where the warring *shugo* had resided for many years, so every mansion now had either to be consolidated into the defensive strategy or destroyed to deny it to the enemy. The Eastern Army's overall strategic plan appears to have been to establish a defensive area to the east of the Horikawa with easy communications between the mansions of Katsumoto's supporters and the vital Palace of Flowers that was located safely to their rear.

To secure this area the Eastern Army would first have to eliminate the hostile Isshiki mansion that lay inconveniently in the middle of their intended sphere of control just to the west of the Palace of Flowers. Realising that the Westerners may have been thinking along very similar lines (as would indeed be demonstrated when they attacked Hosokawa Katsuhisa's mansion that lay within their own planned defensive zone) Katsumoto ordered the fortification of his allies' homes, so ditches were dug and palisades and towers were raised around them. By this action several lordly mansions, many of which were already surrounded by high

THE ŌNIN WAR

walls and ditches since the time of the *tsuchi-ikki* disturbances, became makeshift fortresses or *kamae*. Some acquired names, so that Shiba Yoshikado's fortified mansion was known as the Buei-kamae and Hosokawa Shigeyuki's home was the Sanshū-kamae, while Yamana Sōzen led his army from the Yamada-kamae.[5] *Ōnin ki* notes that the local townspeople, who were unaware of the reasons behind the new programme of fortification, mocked the move, scorning the cowards who had not gone to the assistance of Hatakeyama Masanaga in the Kami Goryō Shrine and were now locking the stable door after the horse had bolted.[6]

A street scene in Kyoto at the time of the Ōnin War is recreated here in the National Museum of Japanese History at Sakura.

The all-out conflict between Yamana Sōzen and Hosokawa Katsumoto which we now call the Ōnin War finally began with the attack on the Isshiki mansion on 27 June, which launched the full horrors of civil strife on to Kyoto. Unlike the Hatakeyama rivals' encounter at Kami Goryō, there was no speedy resolution to the fight. Instead, there began a series of deadly skirmishes which have been termed the battle of Rakuhoku (Northern Kyoto), otherwise known as 'the Battle of the Fifth Month'. It consisted of two days of rapidly moving action that drew in many participants before developing into the situation of stalemate for which the Ōnin War would forever become notorious. It also provided the first instances of the arson attacks on homes and temples that would further characterise the time.

In the midst of its description of the attack on the Isshiki mansion and other local strongpoints (the relevant chapter is ominously entitled, 'Battles in Various Places') *Ōnin ki* includes a detailed list of the initial troop numbers on both sides, providing figures of 161,500 for the Eastern Army and 116,000 for the Western Army. The figures are likely to be exaggerated

---

5   Goza, Yūichi. 2016, p.108.
6   Shimura, Kunihiro. 2017, p.58.

THE FIRST YEAR OF ŌNIN

by a factor of ten, but the names of their leaders may be assumed to be an accurate and their line-up is very interesting. As may be expected, the appearance of familiar surnames in both armies indicates the continuation of the succession disputes that had preceded the Ōnin War, but other clans had split in two when the rival factions coalesced around them, forcing former neutrals to take sides.

For the Eastern Army we note first the presence of the extensive Hosokawa clan under their overall leader Hosokawa Katsumoto, including Shigeyuki, Shigeharu, Katsuhisa, Tsuneari and Mochihisa. With them of course is Hatakeyama Masanaga together with Kyōgoku Mochikiyo, who represented one half of the now divided Sasaki clan; the other half were the Rokkaku who supported the Western Army. Takeda Nobutaka's family were a powerful clan from Western Japan, while Shiba Yoshitoshi represented the pro-Hosokawa faction in a long running succession dispute within the Shiba family. A surprise is provided by the inclusion of the name of Yamana Koretoyo, who had fallen out with his father Sōzen over an inheritance dispute and defected to the Eastern Army. Finally, we note Akamatsu Masanori, the nephew of the man who had murdered a shogun. The clan's restoration to favour had come about in 1457 when retainers of the Akamatsu had settled by force a strange and anomalous development involving remnants of the Southern Court. In 1443 some diehard supporters had managed to steal one of the three items that made up the imperial crown jewels. They found themselves an imperial prince and set him up as a rival emperor in the mountains beyond Yoshino. In 1457 the Akamatsu force located the site of his hideaway and slew the pretender.

On the other side of the Horikawa Yamana Sōzen commanded the Western Army from his base in Nishijin ('western camp'), a place name that had survived prominently to this day; it is now the centre of Kyoto's textile trade. Sōzen was accompanied by many kinsmen, so we find Yamana Noriyuki, Yamana Masakiyo and Yamana Toyouji listed among

The streets of Kyoto that lay between the mansions would have resembled this reconstruction of the castle town of Ichijōdani in Fukui Prefecture.

THE ŌNIN WAR

his prominent commanders. As for his allies, Hatakeyama Yoshinari firmly supported the man who had once encouraged him so loyally. Others showed the results of internal clan divisions: Toki Shigeyori, Rokkaku Yukitaka who had split from the Sasaki, Togashi Masachika, Isshiki Yoshinao and Shiba Yoshikado, the rival to Yoshitoshi in the Shiba dispute.

With the words, 'At dawn on the twenty-sixth day friend and foe drew up their ranks and an exchange of arrows (*ya awase*) began', *Ōnin ki* launches its account of the Battle of Rakuhoku.[7] The mention of arrow exchanges is highly significant because *Ōnin ki* normally prefers to dwell on episodes of heroic individual combat rather than random arrows in its accounts of battles. In reality, as the days, months and ultimately years went by bows would be the most common and the deadliest weapons deployed in the fighting, as is confirmed by several diary entries from eyewitnesses. In his record for 5m 26d [27 June] in *Gohōkōin ki* Konoe Masaie states that, 'there was *ya ikusa* (arrow warfare) all day', and the following day's entry is little different: 'Today more than anything else, it is all *ya ikusa*'. A different source for the same period confirms that, 'In Kyoto every day there is arrow warfare here and there', and a full seven years later on Bunmei 6, 7m 26d [7 September 1474] a monk from the temple of Tōji notes the Western general Ōuchi Masahiro's 3,000 men still relying on, 'arrow exchanges here and there' as their primary mode of fighting, and in another person's diary entry for 9m 9d [19 October] of the same year the expression used to described the exchanges is also 'arrow warfare'.[8] These comments are supported by an analysis of the *gunchūjō*, the petitions for reward to one's superior that include lists of wounds suffered by one's followers. The historian Suzuki Masaya has studied a sample from the first two years of the Ōnin War, and of the fifty-two named wounded, eleven had spear

An archer holding an arrow. Archery warfare by skirmishing (*nobushi*) caused many of the deaths and wounds during the Ōnin War.

---

7   Shimura, Kunihiro. 2017, p.61.
8   Suzuki, Masaya. 2001. *Nazo toki Nihon kassen shi: Nihonjin wa dō tatakatte kita ka* (Tokyo, Kōdansha), p.109.

wounds with five from other cutting weapons, while three suffered stone wounds and no less than thirty men had arrow wounds.[9]

References to archery and stirring accounts of single combat make up the fine details of the early fighting between the Eastern and Western Armies, but the overall course of events is sometimes difficult to understand. This is partly because certain place names mentioned in *Ōnin ki* can no longer be identified with certainty, but the attack on the Isshiki *kamae* can be reconstructed with some confidence. It began at the Hour of the Tiger, 'when a war drum sounded from the main gate and war cries were raised'.[10] Isshiki Yoshinao was not present when his mansion was attacked and burned to the ground. Correctly foreseeing trouble, he had wisely taken refuge with Yamana Sōzen. Along with the burned-out site of his *kamae*, the Eastern Army acquired the nearby temple of Jissō-In and another religious institution called the Shōjitsubō that lay across the Kokawa.[11]

We must assume that the Eastern Army's plan of removing a hostile base from their rear had succeeded with this speedy victory, but retaliation was soon to follow when a detachment of the Western Army under Shiba Yoshikado attacked Hosokawa Katsuhisa's mansion 'on Ichijō-Ōmiya to the south of the Rozanji'.[12] The Eastern Army were probably not surprised by the move and 'gritted their teeth because of the former disgrace at Kami Goryō, so the situation became one of retreat, attack, retreat, attack'.[13] As the fighting grew in intensity Kyōgoku Mochikiyo sent in reinforcements to aid the Hosokawa force, so the latter took the opportunity to rest and quench their thirsts at the nearby temple of Kumonodera.

The Western Army then fought back against the newcomers. 'The Kyōgoku force advanced but could not decide where to give battle. Asakura Takakage, of Shiba Yoshikado's army, jumped down from his horse and killed five or six of them on his own'.[14] This counterattack by the Shiba force proved decisive in driving the Easterners back, and the Kyōgoku troops attempted to retreat to the safety of Hosokawa Shigeyuki's mansion. Unfortunately for them, their escape route lay across the very narrow bridge of Modoribashi that took Ichijō over the Horikawa, and their rush to withdraw caused utter chaos when the fleeing troops became crushed together on the bridge:

> Sons abandoned fathers and followers lost sight of their masters because, not knowing that the Modori Bridge was narrow and dangerous, they all tried to cross the bridge at once. There was a sound like a landslide on a mountain as men and horses fell from the

---
9   Suzuki, Masaya. 2001, p.110.
10 Shimura, Kunihiro. 2017, p.64.
11 Shimura, Kunihiro. 2017, p.61.
12 Shimura, Kunihiro. 2017, p.65.
13 Shimura, Kunihiro. 2017, p.65.
14 Shimura, Kunihiro. 2017, p.65.

THE ŌNIN WAR

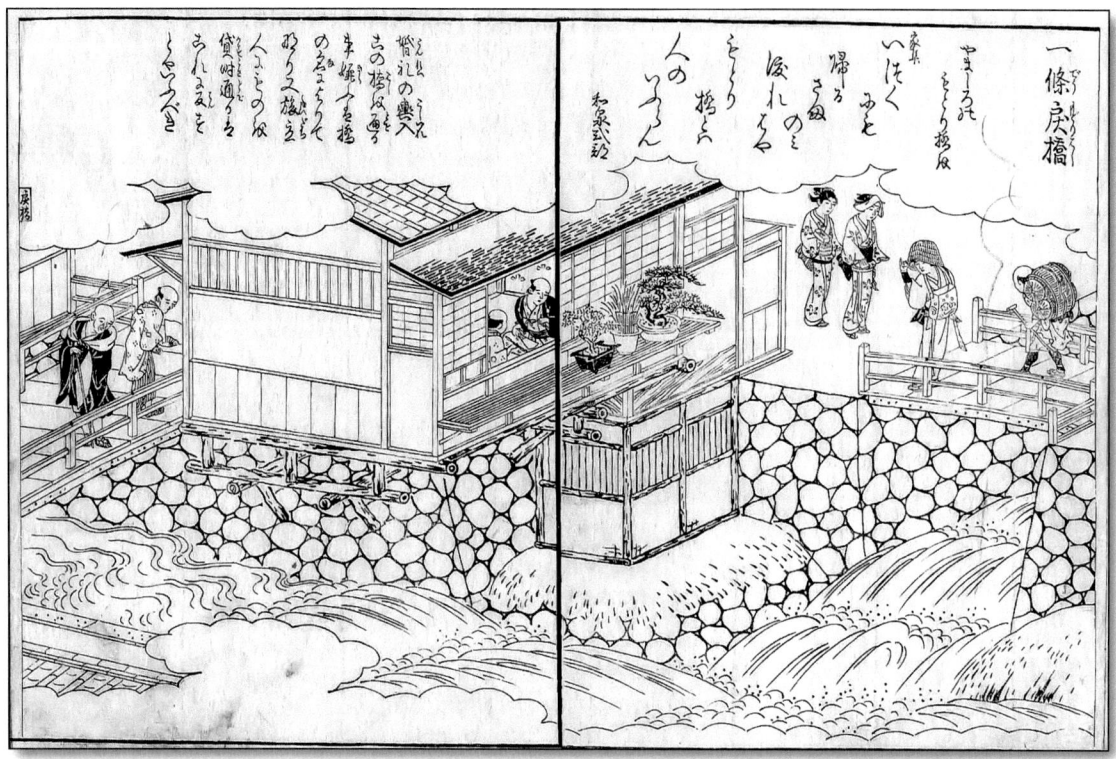

The Ichijō Modoribashi was the narrow bridge that took the avenue of Ichijō over the Horikawa. Kyōgoku Mochikiyo's army became crushed together as they tried to retreat across the bridge.

parapet, and the soldiers who were resting at the Kumonodera were taken aback. "What's happening?" they cried. "Answer us!". Those of the Kyōgoku force who were bringing up the rear had no idea what lay in front of them. The river was so full of bodies that it resembled a level field.[15]

Hearing of this development Akamatsu Masanori tried to assist the Eastern Army by attacking the Shiba, who were made to flee in their turn, but in this case the retreating force found a place of safety. Meanwhile Hosokawa Katsuhisa had escaped to Hosokawa Shigeyuki's Sanshū-kamae. The victorious Western Army burned Katsuhisa's mansion and soon turned their attentions to Shigeyuki's own residence, gleefully setting fire on their way to three important temples: the Buddha Hall of the Hyakumanben Chionji, the priests' quarters of the nearby Kōdō and the Gyōganji.[16] By means of such actions both sides established an early reputation for disordered warfare and seemingly random attacks on property that would characterise the next few months of fighting and haunt their reputations for centuries to come.

One brief passage in *Ōnin ki* provides a rare insight into the street fighting that took place that day. It also compares one samurai's brave deeds

---

15   Shimura, Kunihiro. 2017, p.66.
16   Shimura, Kunihiro. 2017, p.68.

to the exploits of a legendary figure from ancient times who had withdrawn an arrow from his wound and loosed it back at his attacker:

> The Inokuma area in Ichijō-Ōmiya consisted of narrow alleyways where the eaves of the houses overlapped one another on all sides. Attacked repeatedly by fresh troops, Kai Tsuneharu and Asakura Takakage grew exhausted from the fighting and pulled back to the west of the Rozanji. Yamana Sagami-no-kami Noriyuki was waiting for them there, so a further supply of reinforcements now fought at their side. On the Akamatsu side Urakami, Kodera and Satō fought to the last. Among them, Satō Bungo-no-Kami was shot through his left cheek, but he broke off the arrow and held down Yamana Hitachi-no-Kami, a kinsman of Yamana Sagami-no-Kami, cutting off his head and raising it impaled upon his sword. Thus did his name become as famous as that of Kamakura Gengorō Kagemasa from ancient times.[17]

The impalement of a victim's severed head on the point of a sword was the frequent outcome of single combat during the Ōnin War.

Subsequent to the day's destruction, both forces retired. The battle of Rakuhoku had lasted from about 4 a.m. on the 26th day until about 6 p.m. the following day, leaving the combatants 'exhausted, staggering about and unable to breathe'.[18] Writing in *Gohōkōin ki*, Konoe Masaie lamented that, 'It is said that the numbers of wounded and dead on both sides are unknown, but in spite of that it has not proved to be a decisive encounter'.[19] *Ōnin ki*'s version of the events supplements the battle's body count with its disastrous physical results using the following words:

> The mansions of Katsuhisa, Shigeharu and Okabe Katsuyoshi were burned down along with many Buddhist temples, leaving not a single house behind. When the two sides stopped fighting, they both assessed the situation; in the Western lines up to Senbon, Kitano and Saikyō, dead and wounded were all over the place, lying

---

17 Shimura, Kunihiro. 2017, pp.67–68.
18 Shimura, Kunihiro. 2017, p.69.
19 Ogawa, Makoto. 2013. *Yamana Sōzen to Hosokawa Katsumoto*. Tokyo: Yoshikawa Kōbunkan, p.152.

THE ŌNIN WAR

where they had fallen; in the Eastern lines too, you could not walk without stepping over a wounded man or a dead body.[20]

When the 28th day [29 June] arrived, there was no fighting and an uncanny stillness reigned, but fires still broke out in several places. This is confirmed by Jinson, who witnessed the fact that many houses of nobles and samurai, together with temples and shrines, were burned down 'south of Funaokayama and as far as the north of Nijō'.[21] That same day shogun Ashikaga Yoshimasa tried to intervene in the dispute, ordering the warring sides to 'cease fighting for now and await instructions'.[22] His plea was ignored, so the arrow exchanges and fires continued.

In many cases exactly who was responsible for which arson attack would never be known, but this was to become the enduring image of the 'war by fire' of the Ōnin conflict, and the Battle of the Fifth Month began to change in both tone and momentum as the two sides settled down in a number of entrenched positions that utilised the city blocks to their best defensive advantage. The landscape of Northern Kyoto would soon be altered by the new situation, and Ōnin ki describes the scene that would meet the eye after just one more month of this very different mode of fighting:

On 6m 8d [9 July] of the same year, the central gate of Isshiki Gorō's mansion in Inokuma was set on fire by *ranbō hito* (violent individuals), and also the mansion of the chief priest of the Yoshida Shrine in Konoe-machi was set on fire by thieves; furthermore at the same time fires broke out in nine locations, and because a southerly wind was blowing at the time, an area of 100 *chō* was

A suit of armour of *haramaki* style (opening at the back) typical of the Ōnin War. It has large *ōsode* (shoulder plates) and a heavy *nodowa* (throat guard).

20 Shimura, Kunihiro. 2017, p.69.
21 Goza, Yūichi. 2016, pp.89–90.
22 Goza, Yūichi. 2016, p.90.

reduced to ashes, encompassing Nijō in the south up to the Goryō Crossroads, out to Otoneri in the west and to Muromachi in the east, taking with it 30,000 dwellings of nobles and samurai and reducing everywhere to a desolate plain.[23]

The Desolate Plain

This newly created 'desolate plain' was the result of two related factors which began that month: planned construction and equally planned destruction. The planned construction involved the creation of what are frequently referred to in contemporary diaries as 'castles', employing instead of *kamae* the familiar character *shiro* that appears in the name of the most common type of fortification for the age: the mountain castle or *yamashiro*. For example, Jinson writes that, 'major and minor roads were cut through for *shiro* construction'.[24] The resulting fortifications were brought into being by enlarging and strengthening the existing *kamae,* and the finished products must have resembled Ōuchi Yoshihiro's wooden walls at Sakai in 1399. These urban castles took in a set of specific city blocks that enclosed groups of mansions and houses possessed by one side or the other together with adjacent properties within their extended grid, so that the homes of merchants and commoners were inevitably drawn into the protective enclave. To the mansions' existing walls were added even more wooden parapets, towers, ditches and moats to create a series of sturdy fortresses in the middle of northern Kyoto.

The destruction that accompanied the building programme took place in between the *kamae* and was not always the result of wanton damage. Instead, whole city blocks were deliberately burned out to deny a particular location to the enemy or to provide a flat area of land where mounted troops could be freely deployed. The strategic thinking behind the latter process was based on the belief that the greatest threat that bands of mounted samurai archers faced within a city environment came not from other armed horsemen but from *nobushi*, a word that does not necessarily indicate a particular group or class of warrior but can be regarded as a technique. The literal meaning of *nobushi* is 'those who hide in fields' because it was the tactic of archery skirmishing, and it is clear from the literature that all classes of samurai participated. As for defence from *nobushi*, arrows from foot soldiers had always been deadly to isolated mounted samurai, but groups of horsemen could usually overcome scattered sharpshooters unless the horsemen's mobility was restricted by the terrain, hence the emphasis in the name *nobushi* on 'hiding', for which the alleyways within the city blocks were the ideal killing grounds. The drastic solution introduced during the Ōnin War was to slash and burn the areas between the *kamae* so that

---

23   Shimura, Kunihiro 2017, pp.71–72.
24   Goza, Yūichi. 2016, p.107.

THE ŌNIN WAR

the skirmishers had nowhere to conceal themselves. The result was that any arrow exchanges were now more likely to be delivered from fortified positions while bands of horsemen operated comparatively freely in the areas in between, and we will see below how innovative infantry techniques would emerge during the following months to make the best use of Kyoto's terrible new appearance.

The mounted archer was still the backbone of any samurai army, and the empty spaces created within Kyoto by the burned-out buildings gave them room to manoeuvre without being picked off by *nobushi* (skirmishers).

7

Warriors from the West

The most remarkable political feature about the initial encounters between Hosokawa Katsumoto and Yamana Sōzen that took place in Kyoto during the Battle of the Fifth Month is that their relative standing in the shogun's eyes became completely reversed. Before the battle of the Kami Goryō Shrine Yamana Sōzen had enjoyed Yoshimasa's approval. Scarcely six months later – and just a few days after their first encounter – Hosokawa Katsumoto was granted use of the shogun's banner, which he raised in triumph outside the Shizokumon, the 'four-legged gate' of the Palace of Flowers on 6m 1d [2 July]. At the same time Yoshimasa officially commissioned his brother Yoshimi to subdue the Yamana, who now became officially the rebels against both the Bakufu and the emperor. To some extent this change of heart indicates little more than Yoshimasa's persistent fickleness. He had (to his credit) tried to arrange a truce between the warring factions and had gone to the lengths of warning them that the first to attack the other would be declared a rebel. The guilty party in that was undoubtedly Hosokawa Katsumoto, yet somehow Katsumoto persuaded the shogun that Yamana Sōzen should be stigmatised as the true rebel against the throne.

Certain of Yamana's supporters deserted when they heard of these developments, so Hosokawa Katsumoto turned the screw further by stimulating unrest back in the Western Army's home provinces, thus forcing its leaders to withdraw troops from Kyoto. He also moved rapidly to quench any pro-Yamana sentiment that might still exist within the political morass that was the shogun's court. Katsumoto suspected twelve officials in particular, so he surrounded the Palace of Flowers and demanded their expulsion. Secure in the knowledge that Katsumoto would never attack the shogun's palace and eject them the alleged conspirators made no response, and the initiative came to nothing, but Katsumoto succeeded in getting rid of them by a very different route. Hearing rumours that the Western Army planned to abduct the reigning sovereign and the abdicated emperor, Eastern Army troops escorted them from the imperial palace to the safety of the Bakufu headquarters. Faced by this large influx of soldiers the twelve suspects fled.

THE ŌNIN WAR

These machinations proved to be the high point of the Eastern Army's achievements, because later in the seventh lunar month a development occurred that promised to break the stalemate in favour of Yamana Sōzen. Reliable reports reached the ears of Hosokawa Katsumoto that large numbers of reinforcements for the Western Army had begun arriving from Western Japan. They were men whose leaders cared little that their ally had been branded an enemy of the throne, and to understand this development we need to backtrack somewhat and focus on the little-known enmity that had existed for several years between shogun Ashikaga Yoshimasa and the Ōuchi clan.

The story begins with Ōuchi Norihiro (1420–1465), the grandson of rebel Ōuchi Yoshihiro, who had been killed at Sakai in 1399. Norihiro occupied a similar position to that of his grandfather: a provincial lord whose power was growing in such a way as to cause concern to the Bakufu. As a consequence of the Ōei rebellion the Ōuchi territories had been reduced to a few provinces in the west of Honshu on the Inland Sea, but they prospered nonetheless because as the local *shugo* they still controlled the Straits of Shimonoseki and thereby much of the trade with China. In 1465 Yoshimasa tried to curtail Ōuchi influence by confiscating the harbour of Tōsai in what is now Hiroshima Prefecture. No sooner had Norihiro made a military response than he died of illness.

Norihiro's 18-year-old son Ōuchi Masahiro (1446–1495) continued his father's struggle. Yoshimasa responded with an imperial command that the rebels should be crushed, but the Ōuchi were undaunted and blockaded the Inland Sea. This was so successful that no trade passed from Western Japan to the capital by the sea route for the next seven years. Amazingly, apart from one blockade-runner in 1471, the blockade remained in force until 1477, in other words throughout the whole of the Ōnin War period. Nor did Masahiro confine himself to passive measures against the shogun, because in 1466 he attacked other places around Hiroshima. This was a full year before what we know as the Ōnin War began in Kyoto, but even at this early stage the more astute courtiers in the

Ōuchi Masahiro (1446–1495) was the great-grandson of the rebel who had been killed at Sakai in 1399. His arrival in Kyoto altered the balance of power between the Eastern and Western armies. Masahiro's forces would also be the last to leave Kyoto in 1477.

capital had begun to read the signs of the times. Konoe Masaie moved fifty boxes of his documents out of the city for safe keeping in case the conflict should engulf Kyoto.[1]

On 4m 27d [30 May] of 1467 Ōuchi Masahiro defeated the Shōni in a battle at Hakozaki on Japan's southern island of Kyushu. This was a long way away from Kyoto, but in view of the fact that Masahiro's troops would soon be marching on the capital the encounter could even be regarded as the opening action of the Ōnin War.[2] The victorious western armies began arriving in Kyoto during August and September. Ōuchi Masahiro's force must have been considerable, because it is reported to have been conveyed along the Inland Sea on a fleet of 2,000 boats along with a contingent that travelled overland. Eight provinces were represented: Suō, Nagato, Iwami and Aki from Western Honshu; Iyo on Shikoku, plus Chikuzen, Chikugo and Buzen from Kyushu.

The Eastern Army tried valiantly to blunt the advance by severing Masahiro's lines of communication through the ports of Hyōgo and Sakai; a contest that would eventually last for several years.[3] In the shorter term they also tried to destroy the Western bases in Kyoto before the Ōuchi force had a chance to arrive and occupy them. These attacks began on 7m 24d [23 August] at the *kamae* commanded by Kai Tsuneharu and Asakura

A samurai has his helmet knocked off his head by a blow from a fallen rock. The severed rope indicates that this particular stone was dropped from an *ishiyumi*.

---

1   Conlan, Thomas D. 2020, pp.51–52.
2   Conlan, Thomas D. 2020, p.52.
3   Conlan, Thomas D. 2020, p.53.

THE ŌNIN WAR

Takakage. Sadly, *Ōnin ki* tells us neither the names of the places nor their locations, but the fighting must have been very fierce. For example, 'On 7m 25d [24 August] the famous *shugodai* of Kaga, Majima Kawachi-no-Kami, had just fought his way as far as the foot of a tower when the enemy dropped a large stone that smashed his helmet, resulting in killing him'.[4]

Meanwhile Ōuchi Masahiro was making steady progress along the Inland Sea. On 8m 20d [18 September] he breached Kyoto's natural river defences in the Yawata area. Two days later he arrived at the southern tip of the city and then marched proudly into Kyoto itself on 8m 23d [21 September] setting up his first base in the capital within the extensive precincts of the temple of Tōji. A happy Yamana Sōzen rejoiced at his ally's arrival 'as would a thirsty dragon that had been refreshed by water or a tiger sniffing the breeze'.[5] Bolstered by the reinforcements, Sōzen decided to cut the Eastern Army's remaining lines of communication with their positions in the north of Kyoto. His plan, according to *Ōnin ki*, was, 'to drive the Hosokawa side out of Shimogyō, attack their strongholds from the eastern side while defending the imperial palace, set up a position in the temple of Shōkokuji and block the enemy's passage via the Goryō exit'.[6]

The southern gate of the temple of Tōji. This establishment in the south of Kyoto saw much fighting during its history and became the base for Ōuchi Masahiro when he arrived in 1467.

---

4   Shimura, Kunihiro. 2017, pp.72–73.
5   Shimura, Kunihiro. 2017, p.73.
6   Shimura, Kunihiro. 2017, p.73.

WARRIORS FROM THE WEST

In accordance with the first element of their strategy, the Western Army burned out large areas of Shimogyō between Nijō and Rokujō on 8m 23d [21 September]. They now controlled access to Shimogyō from the south, so Ōuchi Masahiro transferred his base from Tōji to Funaokayama on the following day. This boat-shaped hill lay to the north of Uchino, the site of the old imperial palace, which meant that Masahiro was now providing a strong rear guard for the positions of the Western Army. Sōzen then turned his attention to the Eastern Army strongpoints near the existing imperial palace, and the 'attack from the East' mentioned above began.

Ōuchi Masahiro transferred his base to Funaokayama, the boat-shaped hill to the rear of the Eastern Army's positions. This is the view of Mount Hiei obtained from the summit of Funaokayama.

Hatakeyama Yoshinari first set up a position at Tōjiji, a small temple located a few blocks south of the palace. Takeda Mototsuna attacked Tōjiji, loosing arrows into the temple grounds. Yoshinari's side responded vigorously and drove away the Takeda troops, who fled to their own outpost at a temple called Sanbō-In, which was located two blocks east of the imperial palace. Sōzen concentrated his next attack on this place, and on 9m 1d [29 September] Sanbō-In became the scene of a major confrontation as Hatakeyama Yoshinari, Rokkaku Takayori, Isshiki Yoshinao and others attacked the Easterners in the fortified temple with what are said to have been 50,000 horsemen:

> Takeda Mototsuna was a very brave man, but he had only 2,000 men under his command; so, he opened a side postern of the main gate of the Sanbō-In and said, 'Let's defend ourselves and prevent the enemy force from cutting their way in'. From about the Hour of the Hare [6 a.m.] until the Hour of the Monkey [5 p.m.] they drove the enemy back ten times over. Nevertheless, all of them were killed until Mototsuna alone held his ground in defence.

Finally, Mototsuna also fell:

> A huge stone smashed into his three-plate iron helmet, and the impact snapped his 7 *shaku* 3 *sun* long *ōdachi* called Goshoyaki at its *habaki* [sleeve]. Yet even though Mototsuna had lost his sword he made good his escape, uttering a noise like a bellowing ox, and none dared pursue him. Tokoro Gensan was also killed, his eyes and mouth covered in blood.[7]

After this the Western Army set fire to the Sanbō-In and rushed on to attack the greatest prize in the neighbourhood: the imperial palace. The imperial family were of course sheltering in the Palace of Flowers, but a determined attack by Hatakeyama Yoshinari drove away the Eastern guards and yielded an intensely symbolic victory for the Western cause.[8] The outlook was bleaker for Hosokawa Katsumoto's Eastern Army than it had been at any time since the battles for northern Kyoto had begun.

The Battle of Higashi-Iwakura

Throughout this time Ashikaga Yoshimi, Yoshimasa's appointed heir, had been confined to the Palace of Flowers since being escorted there by Hosokawa Katsumoto at the beginning of hostilities. He was becoming increasingly anxious over Yoshimasa's possible decisions regarding the succession, so on 8m 23d [20 September] he left Kyoto for the safety of Ise Province. *Ōnin ki* describes his tedious journey in some detail, and an important paragraph at the start of the account places his flight in the context of the chaotic city situation: '*Akutō* from the Yamana side raided the capital, setting fire and roaming about to steal. Neither friend nor foe dared venture abroad without a small number of men'.[9] The literal translation of *akutō* is evil gangs, which had been a common expression since the fourteenth century for anyone defying authority from bandits to local warriors asserting their independence. In his translation of *Ōnin ki* Varley calls them 'rowdies'.[10] History would call them ashigaru, a phenomenon of the time that will be discussed further below. For now, it is important to recognise that the gangs were not acting on their own behalf as the *tsuchi-ikki* had done but were serving the Western Army in the capacity of irregular troops.

Reinforcements for the Easterners emerged in the person of Akamatsu Masanori, but the Western Army were much encouraged by their recent success and on 9m 14d [12 October] they drove his army completely out of the area of northern Kyoto where most the fighting had so far taken

---

7   Shimura, Kunihiro. 2017, pp.73–74.
8   Ogawa, Makoto. 2013, p.160.
9   Shimura, Kunihiro. 2017, p.84.
10 Varley, H. Paul. 1967, p.177.

WARRIORS FROM THE WEST

place. Masanori fled eastwards to make a stand on the city's eastern side where extensive wooded mountains go under the collective name of Higashiyama. Nowadays the area is dotted with temples among beautiful surroundings that are preserved by the use of tunnels for the modern lines of communication to the East. During the fifteenth century, of course, access through these mountains was solely by narrow passes, and it was the decision of the Eastern Army to make a stand in makeshift fortifications high in these hills. On 9m 16d [14 October] the Akamatsu force set up a position on the mountain overlooking the temple of Nanzenji in an area called Higashi-Iwakura. The focus of the war then shifted briefly to the area of Kyoto around the great Zen temple that had previously escaped the fighting.

The view from Nanzenji looking towards Higashi-Iwakura, the scene of a fierce battle in the Ōnin War.

As the sun went down the Eastern Army cut down trees from the surrounding forest and made large bonfires as a way of intimidating the Western Army into attacking them. *Ōnin ki* notes that these fires could be seen from inside Kyoto.[11] The gesture worked and in the early morning of 9m 18d [16 October] the Ōuchi force attacked from the direction of the Nanzenji. The Western Army should have carried all before them, but it was not to be:

---

11   Shimura, Kunihiro. 2017, pp.76–77.

> The fortresses had been hastily improvised and were not ready, nor were there any proper wooden palisades. If the attack had been launched from all four sides at once, they would have been forced into trying to escape over the Fujiki Pass to Miidera, but when they saw the enemy attacking in individual phases they threw down large stones in defence, and at this the Ōuchi force collapsed and were driven down into the valley bottom.[12]

The piecemeal nature of the Western advance therefore proved to be their undoing. They attacked each Eastern position in turn and in turn were repulsed in a hail of arrows and stones. Thus, the second wave attacked from the Hinooka Pass at Awataguchi, and they too were crushed and driven off. A third wave of troops attacked from the Yamashina direction, with the defenders:

> …crushing them and driving away both attempts, loosing [arrows] from among the trees or from behind rocks. The defeated enemy had the appearance of autumn leaves scattered around a mountainside. At this the Hatakeyama retreated. An hour later Kai Tsuneharu and Asakura Takakage of the Shiba Force, descended from Mount Niogadake, but the valley was deep, and when they reached the bottom they were driven back by thrown stones.[13]

With no enemies left the army on Mount Iwakura realised that they had gained an unexpected victory and returned in good spirits to northern Kyoto. Akamatsu Masanori rejoiced as if 'the dead had been raised',[14] but the Easterners' salvation had a sad ending because some *tōzoku* (thieves) from within the capital set fire to the Nanzenji.[15] So safe had the place been regarded that it had been the location chosen by Konoe Masaie to hide his documents. An *Ōnin ki* says, 'treasures from the capital had been hidden at Higashiyama Nanzenji for fear of it becoming a battlefield. It was terrible that this had occurred so unexpectedly'.[16] It was an ominous warning about how the devastation in northern Kyoto would soon be spread right across the city.

The Battle of Shōkokuji

By the beginning of the tenth lunar month most of Hosokawa's *kamae* had been captured. He still retained the temple complex of Shōkokuji, which

---

12   Shimura, Kunihiro. 2017, pp.76–77.
13   Shimura, Kunihiro. 2017, p.77.
14   Shimura, Kunihiro. 2017, p.78.
15   Shimura, Kunihiro. 2017, p.77.
16   Shimura, Kunihiro. 2017, p.77.

stood out from the local area among the flattened and blackened ruins of its neighbours. Shōkokuji had been Ashikaga Yoshimitsu's pride and joy and had been founded in 1382 because of the shogun's desire to have a prestigious Zen temple immediately adjacent to his palace. It became the Ashikaga family's *bōdaiji* (family temple) and occupied an area of land much greater than that enjoyed by the temple today. On 10m 3d [30 October] Takeda Nobukado of the Eastern Army set up camp within its sub-temple of Shōjō-In to defend Shōkokuji against the expected assault.

This street within the Shōkokuji complex today would have looked little different when the temple became the site of a furious battle.

Determined to capture Shōkokuji, the Western Army bribed 'a wicked monk' to start a fire, under cover of which Hatakeyama Yoshinari and Asakura Takakage led the attack. Their assault succeeded in driving out the defenders, but at the price of the loss of almost the entire temple complex. It burned for three days, although by some miracle its seven-storey pagoda was spared.[17] The destruction touched many hearts, even though the earliest records of Shōkokuji's history show that it had been no stranger to fire. Like all Japanese temples it was made of wood, so a conflagration was an ever-present danger, and Shōkokuji had in fact been completely destroyed by fire within two years of its completion half a century earlier. The rebuilt edifice was again destroyed in 1425,[18] but the 1467 destruction was different. Lightning strikes or accidents were acceptable. Now a warring faction had deliberately destroyed the great Ashikaga edifice in pursuit of their own aims.

The Western attack also had a dreadful human cost. 'There were eight cartloads of heads taken by the Ōuchi and the Toki troops alone. Dead

---

17   Shimura, Kunihiro. 2017, p.89.
18   https://www.shokoku-ji.jp/ (Accessed 15 October 2020).

bodies filled the ditch between the Shirokumo Gate and Eastern Imadegawa. It seemed as if there were tens of millions of them, and more than half were from the attacking side. Among the corpses were some men who were still alive and were trying to climb back up from the bottom of the ditch'.[19] The sight roused pity in at least one breast because, 'There was no one to bury the bodies, but a Zen monk who was known to Katsumoto's son came and buried the corpses saying, "It would be pitiful if these men killed in battle didn't have proper Buddhist funerals, if they can't be buried they will have been treated no differently from dead dogs". An altar was set up next to the Hosokawa field headquarters and a funeral ceremony was held'.[20]

The immediate proximity of the Palace of Flowers to the burning temple (only one avenue separated them) made it dangerous for anyone to remain in the shogun's palace. Tomiko and her ladies in waiting wanted to flee 'to Kurama, Kibune or northern Tanba'. Yoshimasa however, was totally nonplussed both by the panic in his court and the fact that the smoke from the temples and houses blanketed the area in all directions. Instead of fleeing he behaved true to form and threw a banquet.[21] According to a number of diarists, Yoshimasa's wife's fears would be completely vindicated by subsequent events, because half of the shogun's palace eventually went up in flames,[22] although this is contradicted by later reports that the Palace of Flowers survived everything that went on around it until 1476 when it too succumbed to rioters.[23] Meanwhile Rokkaku Takayori, Isshiki Yoshinao and others of the Western Army set up positions within the burned-out shell of the captured temple. Their arrival caused terror among the commoners whose homes lay nearby. 'With the temple burned down, men and women lost heart and their courage disappeared so, carrying children upside down on their backs they rushed pell mell towards Kamo, believing that if they stayed there would be no one to protect them'.[24]

As the embers cooled in the rain the Eastern Army realised that a major possession had gone, but an attempt to recapture Shōkokuji was not long in coming. *Ōnin ki* refers to the ensuing battle taking place 'on the site of Shōkokuji', because the recent devastation had the effect of creating a large empty space where mounted samurai could sweep opponents on foot to one side in the traditional manner. This meant that the Eastern Army would have to contest open ground rather than retaking a series of monastic buildings, so their plans for recapturing the Shōkokuji were based on this new reality. Hatakeyama Masanaga took charge of the operation, and he began by identifying his enemies' positions:

---

19   Shimura, Kunihiro. 2017, p.91.
20   Shimura, Kunihiro. 2017, p.92.
21   Shimura, Kunihiro. 2017, p.93.
22   Goza, Yūichi. 2016, pp.101–102.
23   Keene, Donald. 2003. *Yoshimasa and the Silver Pavilion: The Creation of the Soul of Japan.* New York: Columbia University Press, p.84.
24   Shimura, Kunihiro. 2017, p.94.

WARRIORS FROM THE WEST

He ordered Tōjō Ōmi-no-Kami towards Nishi-Kawabara to intercept any counterattack from the east. That day Masanaga was wearing a black leather *haramaki* with broad shoulder guards and a Koizumi helmet. Dismounting from his horse and taking hold of the shaft of his *naginata*, he gazed towards the East, where 7,000 or 8,000 of the enemy were moving from the site of the Buddha Hall to a position in front of the main gate. They were Rokkaku Takayori's army, and already in position in front of the main gate was Isshiki Yoshinao, while Hatakeyama Yoshinari's force stretched along from the stone bridge in front of the southern main gate.[25]

Masanaga's opponents were very surprised that he appeared willing to take on units of mounted samurai who outnumbered him by three to one, but *Ōnin ki* has him boasting that his innovatory tactics would allow him to overcome 'a million enemies'. The words *Ōnin ki* puts into his mouth are, 'this time it is not just bows and arrows that will triumph', because Masanaga had a plan that represented a revolution in Japanese infantry warfare. Open order *nobushi* archers or spearmen skirmishers would not stand a chance against the Western horsemen, so Masanaga ordered his samurai to advance in dense formations of spearmen protected by heavy wooden shields. *Ōnin ki*'s account of what it calls 'the Battle of the Lotus Pond' continues as follows:

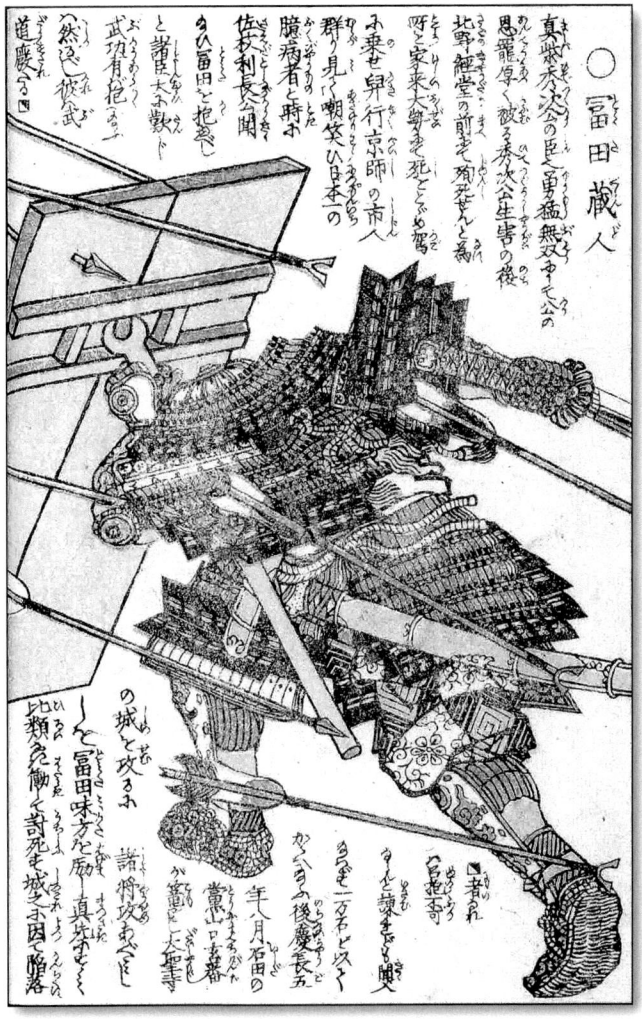

During the battle of Shōkokuji Hatakeyama Masanaga's men advanced on foot behind the protection of large wooden shields like the one shown in this book illustration.

> They lined up with their shields held out in front of them and plunged towards the tiger's mouth that was the enemy. Then, putting to one side the two or three hundred shields, they went in with their spears. … Out of Rokkaku Takayori's force 60 or 70 men who had gone forward fell fighting all together, while their foot soldiers collapsed as if in an avalanche and fled back to the allied lines. Isshiki Yoshinao's unit at the Mountain Gate who came to relieve them were poised to exchange blows with the enemy,

---

25   Shimura, Kunihiro. 2017, p.99.

but they were not aware that the Rokkaku forces had already been defeated by the spears so, thinking that the fleeing Rokkaku side were the enemy advancing against them, they engaged them in battle instead.[26]

Hearing of these developments, Tōjō Ōmi-no-Kami returned to the fray, taking many heads and cutting a way ahead with his sword, but the advancing phalanxes of the Eastern Army had already cornered the enemy and driven them down into the Lotus Pond that lay just inside the southern gate of Shōkokuji. Their legs became trapped in the mess of decayed vegetation and the roots of the lotus plants buried under the winter mud, and more than 600 heads were taken from the Isshiki and Rokkaku forces combined.[27] 'Masanaga went to Tōjō's station and proclaimed with a slight exaggeration, "In retaliation for the eight cartloads of heads taken the day before yesterday at the main gate of the Palace of Flowers I present you with 800 Rokkaku and Isshiki heads. If it's not enough for you, please be patient!"'.[28]

Through the main gate of Shōkokuji lies the Lotus Pond in which hundreds of the Western Army troops were caught and massacred during the battle.

Hatakeyama Masanaga's innovative use of spears had hinted at a future military revolution, although it was a far cry from the tactics that would develop a century later of using large squads of foot soldiers. The samurai spearmen mobilised by Hatakeyama Masanaga may not have been an élite force who possessed horses, but they were clearly valued by their lord and must have been highly trained in order to take a firm stand against a

---

26 Shimura, Kunihiro. 2017, pp.99–100.
27 Shimura, Kunihiro. 2017, p.100.
28 Shimura, Kunihiro. 2017, p.100.

mounted enemy. Nevertheless, Masanaga would soon be forced to abandon his position at the Shōkokuji when Hatakeyama Yoshinari, his great rival from their divided clan, brought up spear squads of his own. The Shōkokuji site therefore changed hands once again.

On 10m 19d [15 November] Ōuchi Masahiro set up a position within the Shōkokuji ruins, but soon withdrew from the desolate space it had become for something more secure. The future lay with fortified *kamae*, not burned-out temples, so both sides allowed Yoshimitsu's grand edifice to become the most poignant piece of no-man's land inside the battlefield of northern Kyoto. As winter set in both sides hunkered down in their lines and delivered arrows and stones to each other across a blackened wasteland through which raids were conducted from time to time, and the First Year of Ōnin moved remorselessly towards its close.

The taking of heads was always a characteristic of Japanese warfare, and accounts of the Ōnin War tell of cartloads of the grisly trophies being collected.

8

The Second Year of Ōnin

Hosokawa Katsumoto marked the beginning of the Second Year of Ōnin in a very precise fashion by reopening hostilities while it was still dark on New Year's Day, 25 January 1468. Unsen Taikyoku recorded the incident in his diary thus: 'In the middle of the night on the first day of this month, Hosokawa Katsumoto's soldiers launched an attack on the Western camp and arrows and stones fell like rain, but when the sun rose in the East they withdrew'.[1] The raid would later be commemorated in a different vein in a heroic poem by the eccentric Zen monk Ikkyū Sōjun (1394–1481):

> On New Year's Day, after crushing the enemy
> Everywhere men raised loud songs of triumph
> A million soldiers of the imperial court
> And not one has lost so much as a single hair.[2]

The brief action is highly unlikely to have been accompanied by any of the poetic elements that Ikkyū includes. It was no more than a short raid against the opposing lines, a tactic which would prove to be typical of the year that lay ahead as both sides settled down into their increasingly better constructed positions. The strongly defensive nature of the war that developed within the epicentre of northern Kyoto in 1468 also meant that the bulk of the fighting would move to the outskirts of the city and to neighbouring provinces. It was almost as if the commanders in the lines were becoming bored by the growing stalemate, which may well be true, because records of the time attest to both the tedium endured by the troops and the

---

1   Unsen, Taikyoku: *Hekizan Nichiroku* (2017 edition). *Hekizan Nichiroku Vol. 2* Edited by Tokyo Daigaku Shiryō Hensanjo. Tokyo: Iwanami Shoten, p.30.
2   As in the translation by Donald Keene in Keene, Donald. 2003. *Yoshimasa and the Silver Pavilion; The Creation of the Soul of Japan.* New York: Columbia University Press, p.68.

THE SECOND YEAR OF ŌNIN

fruitless nature of the fighting that took place around the urban fortifications.

The most important source for the course of the war during 1468 is *Hekizan Nichiroku*, the diary of Unsen Taikyoku of Tōfukuji. His day-by-day entries cover the entire period of the Second Year of Ōnin, and Taikyoku was clearly an eyewitness to many of the events he describes or had personally interviewed some spectator. His observations of the physical environment of the urban war set the scene perfectly and allow us to gain a good impression of the continued enhancement of the fortified *kamae* that had taken place since they were first created. Taikyoku was very impressed by the taller towers that had sprung up to provide observation posts and archery platforms, so we read on 4m 14d [17 May] that, 'Yamana Sōzen built a *seirō*

A sword-wielding samurai. Warriors like this fought throughout the fifteenth century.

(tower); its height was 7 *jō* (22 metres).³ Ten days later Sōzen's comrade-in-arms Ōuchi Yoshihiro built an even higher *daiseirō* to the south-east of the Rokuon-In, a sub-temple of Shōkokuji.⁴ Taikyoku gives more information about it on 5m 27d [17 June] where, 'According to a visitor, if one ascends the Rokuon-In tower there is an uninterrupted view of the Eastern lines.'⁵ The impressive edifice was still dominating the skyline six months later because on 11m 6d [20 November] Taikyoku also notes that, 'The south east *daiseirō* tower is over 10 *jō* high, taller even than the seven-storey pagoda of Shōkokuji that escaped being burned down.'⁶ That would make the tower a massive 30 metres high and must represent the practical limit for such a structure.

---

3   Unsen, Taikyoku: *Hekizan Nichiroku* (2017 edition), p.60.
4   Unsen, Taikyoku: *Hekizan Nichiroku* (2017 edition), p.62.
5   Unsen, Taikyoku: *Hekizan Nichiroku* (2017 edition), p.70.
6   Unsen, Taikyoku: *Hekizan Nichiroku* (2017 edition), p.114.

THE ŌNIN WAR

One important development during the second year of the Ōnin War was the building of tall *daiseirō* (siege towers) as in this reconstruction at Sakasai Castle.

As well as building towers the rival armies heightened the timber and earthwork ramparts around the *kamae*. The materials for the earthen walls came from the spoil extracted by excavating the deep trenches that now surrounded them. As Taikyoku notes, 'The Eastern Army invited Matsuda Hideoki to build deep ditches and tall ramparts, and the appearance of these fortresses cannot be imagined unless you have seen them',[7] but even though the fighting of the Ōnin War is often referred to as 'trench warfare' we must not think of armies standing in slit trenches as in World War I. The ditches were simply barriers to enemy movement, and one built somewhere across Ichijō was massive indeed, being one *jō* (3.03m) deep and two *jō* (6.06m) wide.[8] As for the wooden ramparts, 'On Ōmiya, soldiers held captive by the Western Army collected timber and blocked off the road'.[9]

Within the urban castles thus created the troops suffered long periods of boredom that were enlivened by sudden terrifying raids. For an example of the latter, we note that on 8m 1d [18 August], 'About 100 soldiers from Hosokawa Katsumoto's army infiltrated and attacked Hatakeyama Yoshinari; the sun went down during the thick of the fighting, leaving many dead and wounded'.[10] To pass the time between the raids some of the samurai made little red flags on which they wrote short poems that they themselves had composed. They hung the flags from their belts when they went into battle.[11]

Arrows were the main missile weapons that were exchanged between the lines, just as they had been in 1467, and fire arrows were much used in attempts to set light to rival structures. On 6m 21d [10 July], 'Western Army soldiers attacked an Eastern castle, launching over 2,000 fire arrows, but they did not succeed in setting fire to it and there was rejoicing inside

---

7   Unsen, Taikyoku: *Hekizan Nichiroku* (2017 edition), p.64.
8   Ogawa, Makoto, p.169.
9   Unsen, Taikyoku: *Hekizan Nichiroku* (2017 edition), p.35.
10   Unsen, Taikyoku: *Hekizan Nichiroku* (2017 edition), p.85.
11   Unsen, Taikyoku: *Hekizan Nichiroku* (2017 edition), p.35.

the castle that only 100 men were wounded by being hit from the bows'.[12] Stones were also dropped by hand from the walls. We noted earlier two incidents from *Ōnin ki* when named warriors had their helmets crushed by falling stones, but the fighting of 1468 saw a new – or at least newly rediscovered – way of delivering large stone missiles across the huge gaps created by the ditches. Unsen Taikyoku describes the introduction of the weapons thus:

> A craftsman from Yamato Province visited the lines and constructed *hassekiboku* (stone throwing devices of wood), saying that any location hit by one of these stones would be completely destroyed. As far as the present author knows, devices for throwing stones date from ancient China and were used by Li Mi of Tang, they were called *hō* and were weapons for attacking castles and were also called *shōgun hō*. Furthermore, Cao fired stone projectiles when attacking Yuan Shao's army. They were called *hekirekisha*. In Fan Li's *Art of War*, it says that they can throw a stone weighing 12 *kin* (7.121kg) a distance of 300 paces, so the skills in weaponry known to the Yamato craftsman were not new, and in no way an innovation.[13]

The use of the term *hekireki* (in Chinese *pi li* – thunderclap) poses the intriguing possibility that the *hō* were also used to deliver exploding bombs, which would indeed sound like a thunderclap when they burst in the air over the enemy positions. Unfortunately, the evidence is circumstantial and derives only from the fact that the same two ideographs *hekireki* appear in the name of the Chinese catapult projectiles that Needham translates as 'thunderclap bombs' or 'thunderclap fireballs', which were primarily anti-personnel weapons. They were egg-shaped and made by encasing gunpowder, and possibly fragments of iron or pottery, within thick layers of paper. In one account from the Song Dynasty the thunderclap bombs hit the enemy targets, 'throwing them into great confusion. Many fled, howling with fright'.[14] There are no records from the Ōnin War to confirm them being used in Japan, and the only author to claim that the inclusion of the word *hekireki* in *Hekizan Nichiroku* definitely means exploding bombs is Nakanishi Ritta, who includes a dramatic yet very speculative reconstruction in both his published accounts.[15]

There is however another tantalising entry in *Hekizan Nichiroku* which refers to the use of what are almost certainly gunpowder weapons, because

---

12   Unsen, Taikyoku: *Hekizan Nichiroku* (2017 edition), p.76.
13   Unsen, Taikyoku: *Hekizan Nichiroku* (2017 edition), pp.35–36.
14   Needham, Joseph. 1986. *Science and Civilisation in China, Vol. 5 Part 7 Military Technology; the Gunpowder Epic.* Cambridge: Cambridge University Press, pp.164–165.
15   Nakanishi, Ritta. 1985. 'Hassekiboku' *Rekishi Gunzō*, 17, 2, pp.82–85; Nakanishi, Ritta. 2008. *Nihon katchū shi.* Tokyo: Dainippon Kaiga, p.85.

THE ŌNIN WAR

in his entry for 11m 6d [20 November] Taikyoku notes that, 'in Hosokawa Shigeyuki's lines they have *hihō* and *hisō*, which are used for attacking the towers'.[16] The first expression 'flying *hō*' no doubt means the catapults, but the latter word, which combines the characters for 'fire' and 'spear' is almost certainly a fire-lance, a primitive fire weapon known both in China and in Europe. A device something like a roman candle was attached to the head of a spear. When the gunpowder burned out, perhaps having also spurted projectiles of one kind or another towards the enemy, the blade of the spear was brought into play.[17]

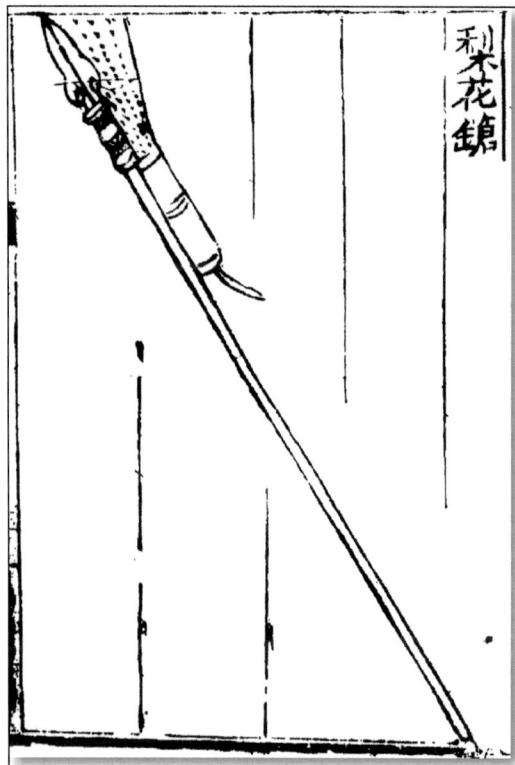

The *hisō* (fire lance) is the only gunpowder weapon known to have been deployed during the Ōnin War.

The fire-lance would therefore appear to be the only gunpowder weapon used during the Ōnin War but, strangely enough, an entry from 1466 in another Japanese monk's diary definitely describes a firearm. The object under description had been brought to Kyoto by envoys from Japan's near neighbour the Kingdom of Ryūkyū (modern Okinawa). In *Inryōken Nichiroku* the diarist notes what he calls a *teppō* being fired during a visit by a Ryūkyūan envoy to shogun Ashikaga Yoshimasa on Bunshō 1, 7m 28d [5 September 1466] and causing great surprise to those who witnessed the demonstration.[18] The Okinawan historian Tōma Shi'ichi has no doubt that the weapon taken to Japan must have been one of the firearms known on the Ryūkyū Islands as a *hiya*, which literally (and somewhat unhelpfully) translates as fire arrow. It was a simple short-barrelled handgun mounted on a wooden stock, and the most popular varieties were three-barrelled. Tōma also sensibly suggests that it was discharged in the capital as a ceremonial salute.[19] There are no records of handguns being used during the Ōnin War, so their military possibilities had clearly not been appreciated in 1466, even though the weapons had been in use on the Ryūkyū Islands for centuries.

Arrows, stones and fire arrows were therefore the normal weapons of distant exchange between the *kamae*, with swords, spears and *naginata* coming into play for close quarter combat during raids. These actions must have been very destructive, but their effects on the built environment were modest compared to the results of the raids launched on non-military targets such as temples and houses. Arson was the main method of attack.

---

16   Unsen, Taikyoku: *Hekizan Nichiroku* (2017 edition), p.114.
17   Described in detail in Needham, Joseph. 1986, pp.240–249.
18   Tōma, Shi'ichi. 1994. 'Hiya ni tsuite'. *Nantō ko-ko* 14, p.124; Uezato, Takashi. 2000. 'Ryūkyū no kaki ni tsuite'. *Okinawa Bunka* 36, 1, p.79.
19   Tōma, Shi'ichi. 1994, p.124 &140.

It was a very blunt instrument, and Taikyoku's list of buildings destroyed by fire reads like a very sad tourist guide to Kyoto as the predecessors of today's familiar landmarks go up in smoke. For example, on 8m 4d [21 August] Western soldiers set fire to buildings of the Shōren-In (the former temple of the late shogun Ashikaga Yoshinori) as well as several other temples, mansions and houses. The following day a clash between rival troops resulted in collateral damage to the Shōgo-In among several other temples.[20] On 9m 4d [20 September] Eastern soldiers set fire to the Ninnaji in Kitayama, and two days later burned down the Fujimori Shrine.[21] On 9m 16d [14 October], the Tenryūji in Saga, the temple that Ashikaga Takauji had founded to console the spirit of Emperor Go-Daigo, was also set on fire. Five days later and directly across the city some Western soldiers set fire to buildings of the Shōren-In for a second time.[22]

The Shōren-In in eastern Kyoto was attacked and burned twice during the fighting in the Second Year of Ōnin.

The rise of the ashigaru

It is in the context of these raids and arson attacks that we encounter the first unambiguous references in the literature to the other great military innovation for which the Ōnin War will always be remembered. This was the use of the irregular troops known as ashigaru, a term that literally means 'light feet'. A century later the word ashigaru would indicate disciplined infantry squads, and a further century after that it would mean the lower ranks of the samurai class, but during the Ōnin War the label 'ashigaru' evoked only contempt. The expression's etymology reflected the observation

---

20 Unsen, Taikyoku: *Hekizan Nichiroku* (2017 edition), p.85.
21 Unsen, Taikyoku: *Hekizan Nichiroku* (2017 edition), p.93.
22 Unsen, Taikyoku: *Hekizan Nichiroku* (2017 edition), p.96.

frequency made during the Ōnin War that these lower-class warriors were lightly protected and would often be armed only with a spear or a sword.

To the rival commanders ashigaru were useful but dispensable. To their noble or clerical victims ashigaru were a curse, a familiar complaint summed up by a pictorial representation of ashigaru on the painted scroll *Shinnyodō emaki* of 1524, where they are shown destroying a building and using their spears not for fighting but to prise up floorboards in search of loot. Their only other offensive weapons are swords, and the group resemble a pirate gang more than they resemble samurai. In another section of *Shinnyodō emaki* an attendant to a mounted samurai who is dressed in simple armour and carrying a *naginata* is placed in the foreground to show the contrast between him as a 'regular soldier' and an ashigaru to the rear who wears only a jacket and has a stolen plank of wood on his shoulder. But where did the ashigaru come from, and why should they be making their first appearance during the Ōnin War?

In previous writings on the subject, I have simply referred to ashigaru as men who were casually recruited into armies in return for the prospect of loot, yet this still begs the question of their origins and the reasons why anyone should wish to become part of an ashigaru group.[23] A very good answer is provided in Jinson's diary, where he identifies these strange new fighting units known as ashigaru, whom he says are also called *ashijirō* ('bare feet'). According to Jinson they are lower class warriors who must be distinguished from samurai, while their violent and predatory activities in battle remind Jinson not of regular fighting men but the members of the *tsuchi-ikki*.[24] The *tsuchi-ikki* phenomenon, which had established itself as almost an annual event prior to the Ōnin War, therefore provides a likely model for the origins of the ashigaru and their deployment by the Eastern and Western armies.

The historian Goza Yūichi agrees with Jinson's ideas and goes further to identify a complete equivalence between *tsuchi-ikki* and ashigaru, noting that the lower class warriors and starving people who had already come together as *tsuchi-ikki* had already demonstrated an innovative military potential that was ripe for exploitation by an ambitious *shugo*.[25] The downfall of certain *shugo* houses before the Ōnin War and as a consequence of it had also led to the creation of numbers of *rōnin* (unemployed samurai), and to add to these two categories of available irregulars there were the *rumin* (vagrants) who had made their way to the capital. These desperate individuals would fight for someone in order to eat, simply because they had no other viable form of employment available to them. With the beginning of the Ōnin War *tsuchi-ikki* rioting had all but dried up, leaving

---

23 e.g. Turnbull, S.R. 1977. *The Samurai: A Military History*. (London: Osprey), p.114.
24 As quoted in the illustrated part work series: Various authors. 2006. *Hosokawa Katsumoto: Yamana Sōzen to Ōnin no Ran*. (Nihon no Kassen Series Vol. 48). Tokyo: Kodansha, p.19.
25 Goza, Yūichi. 2016, p.112.

the battlefield as the only means of expression for these heterogenous mobs who had grown used to violence.[26]

As for their recruitment, the procurement and provisioning of large armed forces was essential for the warring *shugo* in the capital and, as so many examples above have shown, their only source of loyal and reliable troops lay within the home provinces that the *shugo* rarely visited. Fortunately, there was now within Kyoto and its immediate hinterland this ready supply of casual manpower whose skills at raiding, burning and wrecking might now be exploited to achieve the Eastern and Western military objectives, so ashigaru could make up the manpower deficiency as far as their lack of training and discipline would allow.[27] The great weakness of the scheme was of course that the depredations of the ashigaru gangs could never be expected to be confined to the enemy lines but also caused havoc in shrines, temples and noble mansions.

The participants in *tsuchi-ikki* raids like this one depicted in *Hōjō Godai ki* provided a large proportion of the personnel for the ashigaru gangs of the Ōnin War.

To summarise, in the eyes of their victims the only real difference between operations by *tsuchi-ikki* and attacks by ashigaru was that when the ashigaru raided and looted they were doing so by invitation and commission from above. Deploying them was therefore a high-risk strategy, and nothing is more illustrative of the cynical lack of concern for anyone else displayed by Yamana Sōzen and Hosokawa Katsumoto than their willingness to let mobs run riot and damn the consequences.

Ōnin ki introduces the concept of ashigaru, although not the actual word, in its account of an action during the third lunar month of 1468 called the Battle of Inariyama.[28] The operation is also covered by Unsen Taikyoku and concerns a fascinating individual called Honekawa Dōken, who is said to have acted as a recruiter and leader of ashigaru for the Eastern Army. The chronicle tells us that

---

26 Kanda, Chisato. 2002. *Nihon no Chūsei: Sengoku ransei wo ikiru kata.* (Tokyo: Chūō Kōronsha), pp.50–53.
27 Kanda, Chisato. 2002, p.45.
28 Shimura, Kunihiro. 2017. *Ōnin ki.* Tokyo, Chikuma Shobō, pp.116–117.

THE ŌNIN WAR

before the Ōnin War Dōken was employed in the *samurai-dokoro* of the Muromachi Bakufu and that his promotion to *ashigaru-taishō* (ashigaru general) came about because 'he was well versed in the ways of the *tōzoku* (thieves)'.[29] Goza Yūichi believes that Honekawa Dōken is a fictitious character based on a real person called Taga Takatada who probably led the ashigaru unit into battle at Inariyama. Before and after the Ōnin War Taga Takatada was deputy head of the *samurai-dokoro* under Kyōgoku Mochikiyo. This Takatada is said to have hired thieves and *akutō* in Kyoto, so he is likely to have been the model for Honekawa Dōken.

In *Ōnin ki* Dōken's army are described not as ashigaru but as *akutō* and *monotori* (robbers), and its use of the word *akutō* recalls the earlier use of the same word when *akutō* on the Yamana side (Varley's 'rowdies') roamed the capital, burning and looting.[30] We also noted another reference to depredations being caused by *ranbō hito* (violent individuals).[31] Whatever their title, the Eastern Army first deployed 300 of these irregulars under the command of Honekawa Dōken (or his non-fictional alternative) to burn Shimogyō in April 1468 as a way of devastating the Western Army's troop areas and supply routes. The operation succeeded, so Dōken was rewarded with gifts and on 3m 15d [7 April] he was moved to a position on Inariyama. This is the hill near Tōfukuji in the southeast of Kyoto where sits the famous Fushimi Inari Shrine. Nowadays hundreds of vermilion *torii* (shrine gateways) slink up the hill and act as tunnels for worshippers of the *kami* Inari, but in 1468 the only value of Inariyama to the Eastern Army was as a strategic location from which Western communications could be attacked:

Nowadays hundreds of vermilion *torii* (shrine gateways) cover the hill the hill of Inariyama above the Fushimi Inari Shrine. In 1468 it was site of a major battle involving ashigaru led by the legendary Honekawa Dōken.

---

29 Goza, Yūichi. 2016. *Ōnin no ran Sengoku jidai o undo tairan*. Tokyo: Chūō Kōronsha, p.109.
30 Shimura, Kunihiro. 2017. *Ōnin ki*. Tokyo, Chikuma Shobō, p.84.
31 Shimura, Kunihiro. 2017. *Ōnin ki*. Tokyo, Chikuma Shobō, pp.71–72.

Hosokawa Katsumoto presented Honekawa with a bolt of cloth from the Emperor's clothing repository and a gold-mounted sword, and Honekawa moved from Yamashiro to Inari, where he had a consultation with the Chief Priest and set up camp on top of the hill. The men under his command had control of all the roads around including Fushimi and Takeda, and almost all the villages surrendered.[32]

The Western Army's response was to launch an attack on Inariyama on 3m 21d [13 April]. It was completely successful and sent Dōken's casually recruited irregulars fleeing from their positions. Dōken tried to escape by disguising himself in women's clothing, but he was recognised and put to death. A satirical poem would be composed about his rise and fall from receiving fine clothes to fleeing ignominiously. It uses two puns. First, Inari is punned with *hibari* (a swaggerer) and then the couplet makes use of the fact that the two ideographs that made up Dōken's surname of Honekawa mean 'bone' and 'skin'. So (as loosely translated), 'Yesterday he was Dōken the swaggerer/ Today he is wretched, having been reduced to skin and bone.'[33]

Following the battle of Inariyama we begin to encounter words to describe the irregulars that include the familiar expression 'ashigaru'. Unsen Taikyoku first uses the term on 6m 15d [4 July]:

A unit of 300 specially chosen men from the Eastern Army called ashigaru, wearing no armour, with no spears and carrying only one sword each, infiltrated the enemy lines in an operation where they captured prisoners and took heads, and on the night of the eighth day they seized the opportunity to set fire to one of Yamana Sōzen's towers that are six or seven *ken* (about 13 metres) tall. Hosokawa Katsumoto rewarded the group.[34]

This interesting passage implies that the ashigaru were lightly armed by intent so that they could carry out their raids successfully, but that they were also picked troops rather than a casual if deadly mob. They were certainly effective – burning a siege tower was no mean feat – and Taikyoku's passage reminds one of the exploits claimed elsewhere for the troops known as *shinobi*, the skilled infiltrators whose actions gave rise to the legendary ninja. In almost all his other accounts Taikyoku prefers to use the expression *hayai ashi* ('quick feet') for the irregulars, and his account in an entry for 11m 3d [17 November] is closer to the usual notion of ashigaru as casually recruited troops rather than a picked force:

---

32 Shimura, Kunihiro. 2017. *Ōnin ki*. Tokyo, Chikuma Shobō, p.116.
33 Shimura, Kunihiro. 2017. *Ōnin ki*. Tokyo, Chikuma Shobō, p.117.
34 Unsen, Taikyoku: *Hekizan Nichiroku* (2017 edition), p.74.

> Over 300 *hayai ashi* of the Eastern Army went to the great shrine at Uji, and every one of them carried a long *hoko* (spear) or a powerful bow and came skipping and bounding along, wearing on their heads iron helmets or bamboo hats, some of which sported red hair; their thin clothes were of rough hemp, and their exposed flesh showed that they were men who were not afraid of the cold, it was probably their greed that made them have no concern for their bodies, and they moved rapidly along as if they were flying.[35]

The reference to 'red hair' is to the practice of wearing caps ornamented with red horsehair to make the wearer look fierce. The ashigaru could be very effective in their role, because on 8m 2d [19 August], 'a unit from the Western Army set fire to dwellings in Shirudani and during the night burned down the Kōzen Zen-In'.[36] Four days later Taikyoku introduces us to another named ashigaru leader to add to Honekawa Dōken. This was Mizushi of the Western Army, 'who lived in front of the gate [of Tōfukuji], served under Yoshinari and was of an exceedingly good and brave disposition'. Mizushi had command of a unit of ashigaru, with whom he blocked off the Eastern Army's supply routes to Yamashina. This earned the ire of Hosokawa Katsumoto, who was determined to destroy him.[37] Mizushi was however still alive and active on 8m 26 [12 September] when, 'Troops from eastern and western Yamashiro burned down the Tendai sect's Myōhō-In, in addition Mizushi besieged the Hōseiji but did not gain a victory'.[38]

A third named ashigaru leader is introduced on 9m 7d [5 October] in the context of a battle on Funaokayama. The Western Army had enhanced the mountain's natural defences by cutting a ditch around it and raising tall towers. The Eastern Army eventually captured Funaokayama, burning the towers and the outbuildings, but at a considerable price in casualties with over thirty heads being taken and the loss of the leader of the Eastern Army's ashigaru, a person called Koma Tarō.[39] It is with the battle of Funaokayama that *Ōnin ki* uses the word ashigaru for the first time, but the relevant passage concentrates on the exploits of an ordinary ashigaru (albeit one with superior skills) rather than his commander:

> An ashigaru called Ichiwaka who was Urakami's *komono* ('page'), went from Kamo to behind Funaokayama with a mere fifty or sixty men. This was the approach held by Isshiki, who had thought that the enemy would not attack from that direction. Accordingly, almost all his force had gone to Saga and there were almost no fighting

---

35 Unsen, Taikyoku: *Hekizan Nichiroku* (2017 edition), p.113.
36 Unsen, Taikyoku: *Hekizan Nichiroku* (2017 edition), p.85.
37 Unsen, Taikyoku: *Hekizan Nichiroku* (2017 edition), pp.86–87.
38 Unsen, Taikyoku: *Hekizan Nichiroku* (2017 edition), p.88.
39 Unsen, Taikyoku: *Hekizan Nichiroku* (2017 edition), p.94.

men left there. Ichiwaka flew over the ditch and sprang on to the stone and mud-roofed wall and set fire to one side of the *jinya* (headquarters).⁴⁰

Once again we encounter the word ashigaru being used for someone with superior skills, but other ashigaru were neither élite nor successful. On 10m 17d [13 November] a unit of Western Army *hayai ashi* attacked enemies in the Yamashina district but failed to gain a victory and dispersed.⁴¹ The ashigaru incident at Uji noted above also ended badly, because the Western Army got to know of their movements and next day went via side roads and ambushed them on their return, leaving over twenty ashigaru dead.⁴² Sometimes the ashigaru's own greed led to their downfall. On 12m 24d [7 January 1469] an ashigaru unit in the Western Army suffered a self-inflicted disaster. As Taikyoku puts in, 'Some greedy individuals split off from the group, and when the fighting started, they charged ahead of everybody else and all of them lost their heads'.⁴³

In 1471 the Western Army went on a fresh recruiting drive for ashigaru in the Hachijō area of Kyoto. That was where the temple of Tōji lay, so its priests rushed to ban any of the temple's servants and labourers, or any of the people sheltering within its precincts, from enlisting, but the ban was defied.⁴⁴ The life of an ashigaru no doubt had a great appeal for certain classes of society, so the phenomena persisted throughout the Ōnin War into the Sengoku Period, and in 1480 Ichijō Kaneyoshi, a close adviser of Yoshimasa's successor Yoshihisa, would sum up his impressions of ashigaru in *Shōdan Chiyō*, a work intended to guide the young shogun in matters of government:

> Item, for a long time the so-called ashigaru have been something that must be stopped. Since ancient times disorder has attended the realm, but the phenomenon called ashigaru is not a word to be found in the old chronicles… This is the first time ashigaru have appeared and they have gone far beyond being mere bandits. The fact is that their actions have brought about the destruction of many shrines and temples, the ten temples of the Five Mountains, noble houses and *monzeki* [imperial temples] both within Kyoto and in its suburbs, which now resemble places under siege by an enemy who has no respect for any rules. Here and there we are simply crushed, otherwise they start fires and there is the plundering of valuables; these people are nothing but thieves.⁴⁵

---

40   Shimura, Kunihiro. 2017. *Ōnin ki*. Tokyo, Chikuma Shobō, p.118.
41   Unsen, Taikyoku: *Hekizan Nichiroku* (2017 edition), p.101.
42   Unsen, Taikyoku: *Hekizan Nichiroku* (2017 edition), p.113.
43   Unsen, Taikyoku: *Hekizan Nichiroku* (2017 edition), p.120.
44   Ogawa, Makoto. 2013, p.176.
45   As quoted in Various Authors. 1994. *Ōnin no Ran (Rekishi Gunzō Series 37)* Tokyo: Gakken, p.89.

The fighting spreads

It will be recalled that the severe rioting by the 1441 *tsuchi-ikki* had shown that it was possible to cut Kyoto off from its sources of food so, with a stalemate developing between the lines, both commanders switched tactics towards severing the other's supply routes. Such operations were drastic events that could include burning entire villages to the ground. The battles at Inariyama and Funaokayama were both fought with this intention in view, and the fight on Inariyama was a product of the long efforts to secure Yamashina, the district across the eastern hills through which passed the main supply route for the Eastern Army. The Western Army managed to capture it for a while, causing real problems for their enemies in terms of food supplies and resulting illness, but when Yamashina was recaptured the overall situation of stalemate returned.

One alternative available to Hosokawa Katsumoto was to open up an additional supply line through Tanba Province, so certain allies tried to do on his behalf. Much fighting took place within an extensive area called Nishigaoka to the south-west of Kyoto. There were many different land holders there, but the villages who depended on the shared use of water from the Katsuragawa had always cooperated with each other. When danger threatened, they would also resort to arms as an *ikki* under the leadership of the local *jizamurai* as the Nishigaoka-shū ('the Nishigaoka Company') and were able to frustrate entry into Kyoto from Western Japan. With the outbreak of the Ōnin War both armies had to pass through Nishigaoka, so the Nishigaoka-shū were drawn into the conflict either willingly or unwillingly.[46] Many of their members had served the Hosokawa before the war, so they were naturally inclined towards the Eastern Army.

In additional to the military pressure that the Nishigaoka-shū were able to apply, they could also frustrate an enemy by refusing to hand over their tax rice. At harvest time in 1468 the tax rice demands came round again, and by then the warfare had spread beyond Kyoto. At the end of the eighth lunar month the Western Army prepared for an attack on Nishigaoka, so the Eastern Army sent troops in relief and the Nishigaoka-shū joined them. While preparing for military action the Eastern Army began to collect the army rice and in the tenth month more battles took place. The village of Kamikuzenoshō in particular, was made the subject of attack and on 10m 9d [12 November] the Western Army sent in ashigaru to devastate it.[47] They set fire to buildings and looted the rice crop from the fields. When challenged they also succeeded in burning and destroying the mansion of the local leader and Eastern sympathiser, but twelve days later Kamikuzenoshō was recaptured. By way of contrast, in the nearby village of Shimokuzenoshō the stewards and others chose not to resist militarily and instead negotiated with the Western Army even though this course of action was unauthorised

---

46   Goza, Yūichi. 2016, p.113.
47   Goza, Yūichi. 2016, p.115.

by their main landowner the temple of Tōji. As a result of their deliberations the villagers agreed to hand over *hanzei* ('half tax') and thus avoided an attack by the Western Army. It demonstrated that even in the midst of a war people like this could take the initiative and survive.[48]

The 1441 *tsuchi-ikki* had shown that it was possible to cut Kyoto off from its sources of food, a tactic that was tried during the Ōnin War. Much trade arrived by river, as shown by the straw bales on a boat in this reconstruction in Hiroshima Prefectural Museum of the archaeological site of Ashida.

Numerous references in *Hekizan Nichiroku* attest to the spread of operations like these beyond the outskirts of the city in a way that had not occurred hitherto. For example, the Sasaki and Rokkaku rivals from their divided clan fought each other at Chōkōji Castle in Ōmi Province. No defence was offered by the garrison and the castle was destroyed. During the fighting a certain Shioya, a follower of Yamana Sōzen of the Western Army and 'a man of a brave yet unruly disposition', was killed by a flying arrow.[49] On 9m 9d [25 September], as part of their strategy to cut the Ōuchi supply lines from the west, the Eastern Army attacked Ōuchi Masahiro's supporters in Settsu Province and over 300 were killed.[50] A few days later 1,500 soldiers attacked Tanba.[51] During the following month Western soldiers attacked Toba and over 300 were killed there too. So matters continued, and at the end of the second year of Ōnin the *nengō* was changed and the First Year of Bunmei began. The era of Ōnin had finished, but the war of Ōnin had not.

---

48 Goza, Yūichi. 2016, p.116.
49 Unsen, Taikyoku: *Hekizan Nichiroku* (2017 edition), p.62.
50 Unsen, Taikyoku: *Hekizan Nichiroku* (2017 edition), p.94.
51 Unsen, Taikyoku: *Hekizan Nichiroku* (2017 edition), p.96.

9

The Bunmei War

After 1468 there was no significant military activity within Kyoto itself for the duration of the remainder of the Ōnin War. The fortified mansions still stood where they had been built and arrows were still exchanged between them, but the sparring between the two rivals within the capital had now moved largely into the political sphere. There were also fewer soldiers in Kyoto because some of the commanders had started to move back to their own provinces to put down disturbances that had arisen in their absence. Yet the Ōnin War still had an amazing nine years left to run as the fighting continued into the Bunmei era. This chapter will deal with both aspects of the Bunmei time of the conflict: the politicking in Kyoto and the fighting elsewhere which persisted for a decade until neither the politics nor the warfare that had begun in 1467 could be distinguished from the chaos going on around them.

Throughout this time great problems were posed for Yoshimasa by the existence of his once chosen heir Ashikaga Yoshimi. We noted earlier that Yoshimi had fled to Ise in 1467 in fear of his life. During the spring of 1468 Ashikaga Yoshimi returned to Kyoto at the urging of the shogun, but any reconciliation between the brothers proved to be short-lived because a rumour reached Yoshimasa's ears that Hosokawa Katsumoto was planning a coup d'état whereby the shogun would be replaced by Yoshimi. In order to prove the story wrong Katsumoto arranged for Yoshimi to move to Mount Hiei where he might be seen as no threat, but instead of returning to his former life as a monk and going into seclusion Yoshimi was greeted by Yamana Sōzen's supporters who commissioned him as their shogun and made him the nominal head of the Western Army! Faced by the fact that Yoshimi was now the titular leader of his enemies, Ashikaga Yoshimasa performed a complete U-turn and named his four-year-old son Yoshihisa as his newly chosen heir in 1469. He also made the emperor strip Yoshimi of his court ranks and had him declared a rebel, so the final years of the Ōnin War became a struggle between Yoshimasa and his brother Yoshimi over who would be the next shogun.

In a further bizarre development the ever-resourceful Yamana Sōzen went much further than proclaiming Yoshimi as the true shogun and sought support from the highest authority in the land. The background was that throughout the entire conflict Hosokawa Katsumoto had controlled both the emperor and ex-emperor and had made them declare the Western Army to be rebels against the throne, but in 1469 there was a local uprising in the Yoshino-Kumano area in favour of what little remained of the Southern Court. The rebels' candidate for emperor, who would prove to be the last ever nominee for the post, was called Prince Ogura Oze and was a descendant of an earlier Prince Ogura who had been the focus of a failed rebellion in 1428. The southern insurgents had advanced as far as Yamato Province when the movement reached the ears of Yamana Sōzen, who realised that if Prince Ogura Oze was proclaimed as Southern Emperor the young man could give the Western cause the imperial legitimacy it had always lacked.

Sōzen's ally Hatakeyama Yoshinari greatly disapproved of the plan, partly because his own territories were being threatened by the revolt, but he eventually acquiesced and on 8m 16d of Bunmei 3 [31 August 1471] the Western Army took the prince to Kyoto and proclaimed him as emperor. The shogun, however, was not willing to recognise his legitimacy, and when Yamana Sōzen died in 1473 the need for an imperial pretender disappeared and the final hopes of the last ever southern emperor died with him. Poor Prince Ogura Oze was forced to wander the country, and there is a record of the 'Nishijin Emperor', as he was termed, passing from Echigo into Echizen on 7m 19d of Bunmei 11 [6 August 1479], but then he disappears from history along with the notion of the Southern Court. He is said to have settled in Tokinoshima in Owari Province (now Ichinomiya City, Aichi Prefecture) where his supposed tomb stands to this day, still proudly bearing the imperial chrysanthemum.

The grave of Prince Ogura Oze, the last of the southern pretenders, who was enlisted by the Western Army as their own emperor during the Ōnin War.

The war ends

It was noted above that the most significant feature of the final phase of the Ōnin War was its spread to the provinces, but the rationale for fighting was now different in nature from the simple East-vs-West conflicts that had taken place in the earlier years of the war. Some of the struggles were still related to the ongoing quarrel, although several participants had changed sides. Otherwise, Japan witnessed a further round of opportunistic rivalry between neighbours, such as attacks by the Ōtomo and Shōni clans on Ōuchi properties in Kyushu while the latter was still engaged in

THE ŌNIN WAR

the capital. There were also a number of new *tsuchi-ikki*, but an additional phenomenon arose, and it was one that took full advantage of the chaotic situation. This was the seizure of a master's lands by his erstwhile vassal, the process often referred to as *gekokujō* (the low overcome the high), a trend that would receive nationwide expression during the Sengoku Period. In some cases, the 'low' was only one social rung down from the 'high' because the usurper was the *shugo*'s own deputy the *shugodai* whom the *shugo* had entrusted with his provincial affairs while he was living or fighting in Kyoto. One example is Asakura Takakage, whose name has appeared several times above as the loyal subordinate of the Western Army. In 1471 he defected to the Eastern Army and severed connections with his erstwhile overlord Shiba Yoshikane. Within a few years he had gained control of Echizen Province as its *sengoku daimyo* ('lord of the warring states period') and ruled his petty kingdom with little or no reference to the shogun.

There would be other examples of *gekokujō* to come, but by the end of 1472 both Sōzen and Katsumoto had begun to yearn for a peaceful end to the Ōnin War. Katsumoto announced his intention to become a monk, while Sōzen, who had long ago had his own head shaved, contemplated suicide. Both these measures proved unnecessary, because in 1473 both men died. Yamana was seventy at his death and Hosokawa was forty-three. Sōzen's Yamana family passed under the rule of his son Masatoyo. Masatoyo made a truce with the Hosokawa but, in an ironic comment on the power

The grave of Yamana Sōzen. Even though both leaders died in 1473, the Ōnin War staggered on for another four years.

that Katsumoto and Sōzen had supposedly wielded, the war continued because both Hatakeyama Yoshinari and Ōuchi Masahiro kept alive the cause of the Western Army against the shogun. When Yoshimasa saw his traditional support from the Eastern Army growing weaker he began to fear Ōuchi Masahiro in particular when the latter assumed the mantle of supreme commander of the Western Army. Yoshimasa accordingly sent out peace feelers to which a number of generals responded, but not Masahiro, who even resisted a direct order from the shogun to lay down his arms. There was renewed if sporadic fighting around Kyoto, and the former capital of Nara, which had largely escaped the violence, saw a clash between Hatakeyama Masanaga and Ōuchi Masahiro in 1475.

Direct negotiations between Yoshimasa and Ōuchi Masahiro began with the shogun sending a letter proposing peace on 9m 14d (1 October) of 1476. This time Masahiro responded positively and presented gifts to the shogun's officials. Peace looked possible, but nothing concrete happened for months, nor were these overtures enough to sway the two Hatakeyama rivals. On 9m 22d (30 October) of 1477 Hatakeyama Yoshinari's army marched out of Kyoto, not as a gesture of surrender but for an invasion of Masanaga's territories in Kawachi, and the fighting between them was renewed on 27d (5 November). Yoshinari attacked Wakae with great vigour, forcing its commander to flee. In response Yoshimasa stripped Yoshinari of his position as *shugo* and gave it to Masanaga. Yoshinari was now officially a rebel again, but in spite of orders to arrest him his strength was such (he also controlled Yamato) that no further expeditions were mounted against him.

By this time the Ōnin War had only a few weeks left to run, so it would appear that the Hatakeyama rivals, whose skirmish at the Kami Goryō Shrine had launched the war, had been fated to fight its last battle. But as the year moved towards its close Yoshimasa focussed his attentions on Ōuchi Masahiro, whose troops still occupied areas of Kyoto, and made massive concessions to the Ōuchi that Masahiro could hardly refuse. All the lands that had been confiscated from Masahiro's father were to be returned to him. He would also be restored to the post of *shugo* of Suō, Nagato, Buzen and Chikuzen and would get back the distant ports where the first conflicts of the Ōnin War had taken place.[1] The generosity of the offer demonstrates how eager Yoshimasa must have been for peace, even though the settlement had to be portrayed officially as a surrender and retreat by Masahiro, who had certainly had a good war.

The retreat was easier to fake than the surrender, because on 11m 11d [16 December], the day after the final agreement was reached, Masahiro left Kyoto in some style. His final act was to let his ashigaru loose to burn down their now unwanted fortifications. As Murdoch puts it so stirringly, 'the sky around Kyoto was ruddy with the glare of the blazing cantonments the Yamana men were abandoning. On the morrow it was found that they

---

1   Conlan, Thomas D. 2020, pp.56–57

had vanished; and the long and disastrous struggle around Kyoto was at an end'.²

The dramatic departure from Kyoto of Ōuchi Masahiro's forces on 16 December 1477 is conventionally regarded as the moment when the Ōnin War ended. If the war is solely defined by the fighting in Kyoto, then this was indeed the case, but conflict continued elsewhere and eventually merged into the wars of the Sengoku Period. Unsurprisingly, an early example of continuity was provided by the Hatakeyama, who restarted their war in Kawachi in January 1478 and would return to the fray again five years later. Indeed, in spite of the deaths of both Yoshinari and Masanaga hostilities between the factions would only cease in 1499.

Back in Kyoto the destruction they and the other armies had left behind was visible everywhere, and the last but one chapter of *Ōnin ki*, which is ominously entitled 'The Burning of Rakuchū', begins with the words: … 'because of the War of Ōnin [Kyoto] became red earth'.³ A long list follows of the city's destroyed buildings and ends with a melancholy image whereby 'the water wheel of the Rinsenji has stopped turning and the site of ancient Saga has become a grassy field'. The chronicler then adds a passage that would reverberate down the centuries:

> The City of Flowers, which we thought would last for a thousand years, has now become the lair of the fox and the wolf. Even the little that is left between Tōji and Kitano has been reduced to ashes and earth, and although there have been risings and fallings in the past, it is lamentable that in this disturbance of Ōnin the Law of the Buddha has been destroyed, and all the religious sects have passed away.⁴

Ōnin had been a war without heroes and – to all intents and purposes – a war without a proper ending. Instead (in Kyoto at least) it seems to have faded into nothingness from sheer exhaustion, and *Ōnin ki* continues by quoting the words Iinō Tsunefusa (1422–1485), who wrote a poem that would be quoted for years to come as a way of summing up the terrible Ōnin War:

> The city you once knew
> Is now a bare field
> And sparrows are seen
> Among the evening clouds
> As tears fall.⁵

---

2   Murdoch, Sir James. 1925, p.617.
3   Shimura, Kunihiro. 2017, p.132.
4   Shimura, Kunihiro. 2017, p.137.
5   Shimura, Kunihiro. 2017, p.138.

The Silver Pavilion

The pages above have shown that several decades of fighting all over Japan had demonstrated that the Ōnin War was not a unique time of strife in the middle of a peaceful century. As Thomas Conlan has argued using his alternative chronology, it merged with other disputes both at its beginning and its end, but what made the Ōnin War special and particularly terrible was the fact that it was fought within Kyoto. Other places on the outskirts may have been destroyed and Kamakura suffered repeated attacks during the same period, but it is the wanton destruction of the capital that never ceases to stir the emotions.

Daihōonji, popularly known as Senbon Shakadō owing to its location adjacent to the historic avenue of Senbon, is the only temple to have survived within the area of northern Kyoto that suffered the bulk of the fighting during the Ōnin War. Most of the places lamented by Iinō Tsunefusa would soon be rebuilt, but something more remarkable than replacement religious buildings would emerge from the ashes of the Ōnin War, because Japan witnessed an artistic and cultural renaissance that will be forever associated with shogun Yoshimasa and a modest little building known as the Silver Pavilion.

The Silver Pavilion (Ginkaku) lies on the eastern hills of Higashiyama across the city from Yoshimitsu's Golden Pavilion on the hills of Kitayama. It is one building among several that constituted Yoshimasa's retirement villa and is his enduring monument, but unlike his grandfather's Golden Pavilion that gleams in the sun's rays, it remains in the shadows of the eastern hills for most of the day and there are no traces of silver to be seen. The building is therefore the perfect expression of Yoshimasa's time, although not for the reasons that are usually assumed. Most tourist brochures state that Yoshimasa intended to cover it in silver in imitation of his grandfather's edifice but could not afford the cost because of the Ōnin War. It is more likely that a silver coating was never intended, and in fact the name Silver Pavilion only dates from Edo Period when the discovery of traces of lacquer on the building during restoration may have let to the idea, but the sheen of its reflection in the adjoining pond is silver enough. After Yoshimasa's death in 1490 the villa complex was consecrated as a Zen temple and called Jishōji, a name and status it has kept to this day, even though the place is almost always referred to as Ginkakuji, the temple of the Silver Pavilion.

Having spent most of the Ōnin War in the Palace of Flowers Yoshimasa had moved temporarily to Hosokawa Katsumoto's mansion in 1471, possibly because the shogun's palace was becoming overcrowded by fleeing members of the imperial household.[6] In spite of all Kyoto's conflagrations, the Palace of Flowers survived everything that went on round it until 1476

---

6 Stavros, Matthew. 2006. 'Building Warrior Legitimacy in Medieval Kyoto'. *East Asian History*, 31, p.26.

when fires started by rioters spread to its buildings.⁷ Yet Yoshimasa never returned to his ancestral home, and was still residing at the Kokawa Palace (as the Hosokawa mansion was then called) in 1473 when he formally passed on the post of shogun to his son Yoshihisa. But in 1481 Yoshimasa quarrelled with his wife. That had happened many times before, but this time he left her and moved temporarily to Iwakura in the Higashiyama district. His departure from urban Kyoto proved to be a liberation. In spite of having lived in palaces surrounded by extensive gardens containing strangely shaped rocks and trees, Yoshimasa had always yearned for rural authenticity, and on Higashiyama he felt at home.

Yoshimasa had been contemplating a permanent move to Higashiyama from as early as 1460, and while the Ōnin War was still raging he had selected a piece of land on account of the peace and beauty of its location. The site also had melancholy associations because a temple called Jōdoji had stood there before being burned down during the Ōnin War. Yoshimasa's heir and rival Ashikaga Yoshimi had been Jōdoji's abbot, and following its destruction Enryakuji had earmarked the abandoned lot for a new cemetery.⁸ Great beauty and poignancy therefore came together to create a space that was ideally suited for 'an aesthetic equipoise to political decline'.⁹ Yoshimasa overruled the wishes of Enryakuji and acquired the site so that he could exploit its qualities by giving expression to the aesthetic principles of *wabi* and *sabi*, the notions of being understated and possessing fading glory. He would succeed admirably, and the most remarkable result of the Ōnin War is that within a few years of contemplating blackened ruins Ashikaga Yoshimasa, the shogun whose misrule and self-absorption had brought the war about, would go on to inspire a cultural revival.

The building of the Higashiyama retreat began in February 1482, and Yoshimasa's living quarters were finished within a year. No public spaces were included in the plans; it was just a private residence for the retired shogun. The Silver Pavilion, which is officially called the Kannondō and was still unfinished when Yoshimasa died, is a modest little building compared to the Golden Pavilion that had provided its inspiration.¹⁰ It is believed to be of exactly the same appearance as when Yoshimasa last saw it, and its unfinished quality is the key to its artistic and historical significance. In spite of its dedication to Kannon the Goddess of Mercy the pavilion was not intended for any specific religious use. Instead, its function was to provide a place from which Yoshimasa could gaze out on the gardens, an activity which could itself be a religious experience.¹¹

---

7   Stavros, Matthew. 2006, p.26.
8   Keene, Donald. 2003. *Yoshimasa and the Silver Pavilion: The Creation of the Soul of Japan.* New York: Columbia University Press, p.130
9   Hayashiya, Tatsusaburō. 1977. 'Kyoto in the Muromachi Age', in Hall, John W. & Toyoda, Takeshi (Eds.) *Japan in the Muromachi Age.* Berkeley: University of California Press, p 22.
10 Keene, Donald. 2003, pp.87–90.
11 Keene, Donald. 2003, p.136.

That perhaps provides a further key to its modesty and restraint; it was for looking from, not looking at.

The result was that our final image of the terrible Ōnin War is Yoshimasa presiding over developments in the tea ceremony, poetry, ink painting and Noh theatre in his Higashiyama retreat.[12] This aspect of Yoshimasa's career is discussed in great detail in Donald Keene's biography of him, which provides a considerable counterbalance to the usual condemnation of Yoshimasa as the shogun who fiddled while Kyoto burned. Keene writes, 'The Higashiyama era was one of the most brilliant periods of Japanese cultural history, and the guiding spirit was the same Yoshimasa who had been a failure in everything else he did'.[13] He continues, 'We may even be tempted to conclude that no man in the history of Japan had a greater influence on the formation of Japanese taste. This was his sole, but very important, redeeming feature. The worst of the shoguns was the best, the only one to leave a lasting heritage for the entire Japanese people'.[14]

---

12   Keene, Donald. 2003, p.139.
13   Keene, Donald. 2003, p.98
14   Keene, Donald. 2003, p.166

10

The Road to Sengoku

Ashikaga Yoshihisa (1465-1489) was the successor of Yoshimasa and proved to be a leader in the style of Yoshimitsu. Unfortunately for Japan he died on campaign against Rokkaku Takayori.

Of all the remaining shoguns who were to reign before the end of the Ashikaga Bakufu in 1568 Yoshihisa, Yoshimasa's son and heir and the ninth of the dynasty, was the only one who showed any evidence of being a descendant of the great Yoshimitsu. Yoshihisa was independently minded even as a child, and in one example of his acumen he had demonstrated to his scornful father Yoshimasa that he too could learn to write good poetry. To Arai Hakuseki, the fact that he was also willing to condemn Yoshimasa's shortcomings was ample grounds for him to be regarded as the best of the Ashikaga shoguns.[1] In this Yoshihisa benefitted greatly from the good advice of Ichijo Kaneyoshi, who presented the shogun with *Shōdan Chiyō* in 1480, which was quoted earlier for its wise words about the curse of the ashigaru.[2]

Intelligent and brave, Ashikaga Yoshihisa led armies into battle in a way that had not been seen since the siege of Sakai. Sadly for Japan, he died on campaign against Rokkaku Takayori of Ōmi Province in 1489. Takayori had been so aggressive against his neighbours that Yoshihisa launched a campaign against him called the Chōkyō no Ran. The shogun's invading forces set up a base at Magari, where they were assaulted by unexpected night attacks by Takayori's allies from Iga Province and the district of Kōka. These operations against Yoshihisa have since been exaggerated out of all proportion because they are commonly

---
1 Ackroyd, Joyce (Trans.). 1982, p.261.
2 Keene, Donald. 2003, p.85.

regarded as the first recorded action by ninja. The Kōka men certainly used surprise hit and run tactics to disrupt the Shogun's invasion, and twenty-one families from Kōka were officially honoured by the Rokkaku for their unconventional part in the conflict. *Ōmi Onkoroku* of 1684 described it as the first operation by 'the Iga-Kōka *shinobi no shū*' who 'proved themselves in front of huge armies assembled from all over Japan'.[3]

Ninja or not, Rokkaku Takayori's campaign was by no means the only disturbance in the years after the Ōnin War, and one other stands out as an illustration of the futility of the previous decade's fighting. It was carried out by the rivals from the Hatakeyama family who had launched the conflict with the battle of the Kami Goryō Shrine and were still fighting each other the year after the Ōnin War ended. We last heard of them in Kawachi in 1478. Four years later they started campaigning again, and it is interesting to note the involvement of the new deputy shogun Hosokawa Masamoto (1466–1507), who was the son of the late Hosokawa Katsumoto and the undoubted heir of his father in the ways of intrigue.

Hatakeyama Masanaga left Kyoto to challenge Yoshinari during the summer of 1482. He was accompanied on his expedition by Hosokawa Masamoto, who eventually brokered a deal with Yoshinari over the possession of certain disputed districts, but Masanaga continued his campaign against his adopted brother. Yoshinari hit back and defeated Masanaga in Kawachi. He then pressed on into Yamashiro, and by 1483 Masanaga's army had been driven back towards Kyoto across the Uji bridge, which he destroyed as a way of hindering the pursuit. A series of engagements around the river basin to the south of Kyoto continued, and towards the end of the year Yoshinari captured the strategically important Inuta Castle, resulting in a stalemate.

As usual a military campaign had paid no regard to the lives of the ordinary people through whose villages it passed. In addition to the normal burning and destruction, some of which was done by ashigaru taken on by the rival armies, local people were captured and forced to work as labourers and porters or had money extorted from them to avoid such treatment. The Hatakeyama armies had also consumed great amounts of food from the local population, so by the twelfth lunar month of 1485 the *jizamurai* of Yamashiro Province had had enough and withdrew their men from both armies to create a fortified camp of their own. Such was the force of the mutiny that the fighting between the two Hatakeyama rivals was brought to an abrupt conclusion, but the *ikki* were not content with making peace between samurai. Instead, they issued three demands: that both the Hatakeyama armies withdraw from Yamashiro; that all lands seized by the military be restored to their rightful owners, and that all barriers erected by the Hatakeyama should be removed. All these points were agreed, and the two Hatakeyama armies withdrew. On 2m 13d [18

---

3   Shimizu, Noboru. 2008. *Sengoku ninja retsuden*. Tokyo, Kawade Shobo Shinsha, pp.186–190.

THE ŌNIN WAR

March] of 1486 a group of 36 leading *jizamurai* assembled at the historic Byōdō-In at Uji to decide how they were going to govern Yamashiro Province without interference from their betters. This they managed to do successfully for the next eight years.

In 1485 the Byōdō-In at Uji became the scene for an historic meeting between the leaders of the *jizamurai* of Yamashiro after they had ousted the Hatakeyama forces from their province. Yamashiro was self-governed for the next eight years.

The Meiō Coup

Following the untimely death of Yoshihisa, the Ashikaga shoguns increasingly became the puppets of powerful outside interests, and it may be argued that the incident that marks the irreversible decline of the Ashikaga Bakufu and the beginning of the Sengoku Period is neither the murder of shogun Yoshinori nor the Ōnin War but an event that occurred during the Second Year of Meiō (1493). Unusually, it is not distinguished by using the word *ran* but is known as the Meiō no Seihen, a word that can indicate a simple change of government or something more serious: in other words, a coup d'état. And a coup is precisely what it was, which made the Meiō affair very different from the Ōnin War. It was directed against the tenth Ashikaga shogun Yoshitane and used his cousin Yoshizumi as a tool. The latter would eventually become the eleventh Ashikaga shogun before being deposed himself.

The background to the coup lay in the untimely death of shogun Yoshihisa at Magari and the need for the retired shogun Yoshimasa to choose his son's successor. Yoshimasa's brother Yoshimi, who was currently in self-imposed exile in Mino Province, was ruled out because he had served as the titular leader of the Western Army during the latter part of the

Ōnin War. Yoshimasa favoured Yoshimi's son Yoshitane as his heir in spite of the taint of association with his father, but in what looked like a re-run of the Ōnin War situation other leading figures backed Yoshizumi, who was the son of Yoshimasa's brother Ashikaga Masamoto. Yoshizumi's supporters included deputy shogun Hosokawa Masamoto, who was again causing trouble in the great Hosokawa family tradition. Despairing at the decision he had to make, Yoshimasa felt that despite increasing ill health and a lack of interest in politics, he had no choice but to abandon his retirement and resume the post of shogun. Construction therefore began on an additional building at Higashiyama from where he might conduct official business, but Yoshimasa's health was growing steadily worse. Its deterioration was first blamed on the unlucky yin-yang direction of the new building, so the structure was torn down, but Yoshimasa's health did not improve.

Ashikaga Yoshitane (1466–1523) was ousted from his post in the Meiō Coup and became a fugitive until being restored to power as a puppet in the hands of the Ōuchi. This would become the pattern for the remainder of the rule of the Ashikaga Bakufu.

Late in 1489 Yoshimi and Yoshitane dared to visit Yoshimasa on Higashiyama. The diplomatic Yoshimi turned up in Buddhist robes as proof that he had abandoned any thought of becoming shogun. Much impressed by this gesture, the ailing Yoshimasa adopted Yoshitane as his successor. A month later Yoshimasa fell into a coma and died on 1m 7d [27 January] of 1490. Yoshitane accordingly became the tenth Ashikaga shogun at the age of twenty-five.[4] His father Yoshimi withdrew to a monastery and was given a high-ranking court title, but he too died within months of his brother. On 7m 5d [24 July] Yoshitane was formally appointed as shogun, but such were the times that he was destined to reign twice, from 1490 to 1493 and again

---

4 Keene, Donald. 2003, p.165.

THE ŌNIN WAR

from 1508 to 1521, with the hiatus being made up by the reign of his cousin Yoshizumi, who took office as a result of the Meiō Coup.

Hosokawa Masamoto (1466–1507) was the son of the late Hosokawa Katsumoto and the true heir of his father in the ways of intrigue. He manipulated two shoguns and was eventually murdered.

There was little hint of the trouble that lay ahead when Yoshitane's reign began, because his behaviour suggested that he might be another vigorous military leader like Yoshihisa. He started where his predecessor had left off and went to war against Rokkaku Takayori, setting up camp at the temple of Miidera. The new shogun received considerable support and was convincingly victorious, but the move had not been backed by Hosokawa Masamoto who still favoured replacing Yoshitane by Yoshizumi. Yoshitane's next target was Hatakeyama Yoshitoyo, the son of the late and very troublesome Hatakeyama Yoshinari, who had continued his father's seemingly endless struggle after Yoshinari's death in 1491. In this latest phase of the Hatakeyama dispute shogun Yoshitane accompanied Masanaga into battle in 1493. They left the capital on 2m 15d [2 March] and surrounded the Hatakeyama strongpoints towards the end of the month. Yoshitane's ultimately successful campaign was a further feather in the young shogun's cap, but once again a military expedition had been disapproved of by his deputy Hosokawa Masamoto. Fearing for his own influence if the Hatakeyama were reunited, Masamoto continued to support Hatakeyama Yoshitoyo after the latter's defeat.[5]

---

5   Ackroyd, Joyce (Trans.). 1982, pp.268–269.

On 4m 23d [8 May] the Meiō Coup – an operation reminiscent of the worst excesses of the Ōnin War – began by Hosokawa Masamoto taking Yoshizumi into his protection and ordering his men to march against the mansions of Yoshitane's supporters. He also attacked the temples where Yoshitane's younger brother and sister were residing, and the brother was killed. Hosokawa Masamoto then took over Kyoto with the support of Yoshimasa's widow Hino Tomiko, formally deposing Yoshitane and proclaiming Yoshizumi as shogun. By this time most of the warring daimyo who had been fighting elsewhere had returned to Kyoto and almost all of them fell in behind Yoshizumi except for Hatakeyama Masanaga, who took the dispossessed Yoshitane under his protection in Shōgakuji Castle in Kawachi Province. Hosokawa Masamoto laid siege to the castle, and when it fell Hatakeyama Masanaga, one of the last survivors of the Ōnin War, committed suicide. His son Hisanobu fled, but shogun Yoshitane surrendered meekly and submitted himself to a fate at the hands of the besieging forces. He was imprisoned for less than two months before being spirited away to Etchū Province by determined supporters. From there he issued a call to arms, and an attack on Etchū by Hosokawa Masamoto was vigorously resisted.

During the stand-off the sons of the two late Hatakeyama rivals kept up the hostilities in memory of their fathers. In the second lunar month of 1499 Hisanobu's forces killed Yoshitoyo to avenge Masanaga in the final phase of the long Hatakeyama rivalry that had given birth to the Ōnin War. Masamoto's key Hatakeyama ally was no more, and later in 1499 Hatakeyama Hisanobu and shogun Yoshitane coordinated a two-pronged attack on Kyoto, but Hosokawa Masamoto attacked Yoshitane's base on Mount Hiei and burned down many buildings before he could reclaim his throne. Utterly routed, Yoshitane fled to the far tip of Honshu and the protection of Ōuchi Yoshioki, son of Masayori and the fourth leader of the family in just over a century to exert influence on the shogun.

This time the Ōuchi decided to support the Ashikaga rather than undermine their authority. They bided their time for almost a decade, and in 1507 the troublesome Hosokawa Masamoto was fortuitously assassinated in his bath by a rival over a succession dispute within the Hosokawa family. It was an ignominious end for a man who was nicknamed 'the half shogun' and had exerted a level of power that his late father could only have dreamed of during the Ōnin War. Masamoto's death paved the way for Yoshitane's return, so in 1508 Ōuchi Yoshioki marched against the capital and inflicted a defeat upon the Hosokawa forces. Yoshitane was restored to power and the alternative shogun Yoshizumi fled after a reign of fifteen years. Ōuchi Yoshioki stayed on in Kyoto as the puppet shogun's protector and controller, a situation that was to be repeated under different puppeteers for the remaining sixty years of the Ashikaga Bakufu's existence.

The Meiō Coup of 1493 had displayed a total change of attitude towards the shogun that would persist until the Ashikaga Bakufu was eliminated by Oda Nobunaga in 1568. During the Ōnin War the claims put forward by the rival leaders concerning the relative rights of Yoshimi or Yoshihisa had never been transformed into an armed usurpation of Yoshimasa or the elimination of one of the cousins, but in 1493 one shogun was exchanged for another, and so it went on until Nobunaga chose not to set up a replacement.

The last of the Ashikaga princes

The alternation of Yoshitane and Yoshizumi in the post of shogun shows clearly that the once all-powerful military dictator had become a mere plaything in the hands of others, and a depressing feature about the fighting described above is the familiarity of the names of the puppeteers: Hosokawa, Hatakeyama and Ōuchi. One important characteristic of the ensuing Sengoku Period was the appearance of new names with unfamiliar pedigrees. Very important developments in this regard took place in the Kantō, but to explain the changing situation in the East it will be necessary to backtrack a few years to the heyday of the Kamakura Kubō.

It will be recalled that when the 'Lottery Shogun' Ashikaga Yoshinori's greatest enemy, the defiant Prince of Kamakura Mochiuji, was killed in 1439 his cause was taken up by the Yūki family, who sheltered Mochiuji's surviving children until the fall of Yūki Castle in 1440. Two of them were captured and put to death, but one escaped and would grow to maturity as Ashikaga Shigeuji (1434–1497). For the next ten years the Uesugi held sway in Kamakura and, in a clumsy attempt to win it back for the Ashikaga, shogun Yoshimasa appointed Shigeuji as Kamakura Kubō in 1449. Unfortunately for Shigeuji, Yoshimasa did not entirely trust him and as was customary, appointed a member of the Uesugi family to act as Shigeuji's deputy with the title of Kantō Kanrei. It was the same formula that had failed a century earlier, and to make matters worse the appointee — Uesugi Noritada — was the son of the man who had brought about the death of Shigeuji's father!

Ashikaga Shigeuji harboured understandable thoughts of revenge against the Uesugi, and his hatred for the deputy who had been foisted upon him was further intensified by the negative reports Noritada was sending back to Kyoto concerning Shigeuji's conduct. In 1454 Shigeuji sent allies from the Yūki and Satomi families to attack Noritada's mansion and Noritada was killed, at which the extensive Uesugi clan combined their branches to conduct a war against Shigeuji. They captured Kamakura and Shigeuji was forced to take refuge in Koga in Shimōsa Province, where he settled for the consolation prize of the title of Koga Kubō ('Prince of Koga'). That was the beginning of the Kyōtoku no Ran, Eastern Japan's so-called 'Thirty Years' War'.[6]

To add to Shigeuji's woes, back in Kyoto his actions were inevitably regarded as a rebellion against the Bakufu because they had appointed his late deputy. In 1459 shogun Yoshimasa, still desperate to retake Kamakura

---

6   Minegishi, Sumio. 2017.

from the Uesugi while reining in the Koga Kubō who had failed so spectacularly, sent his brother Ashikaga Masatomo in a further attempt to impose Bakufu rule over Kamakura. The plan was that Masatomo would oust both sources of opposition and become the new Kamakura Kubō, yet such was the support for Shigeuji and so widespread was the chaos in the Kantō that poor Masatomo never got further east than the castle of Horigoe in Izu Province. Frustrated at not being able to secure Kamakura, Masatomo imitated the dispossessed Shigeuji and set himself up in Horigoe Castle in Izu Province under the title of the Horigoe Kubō. The notion of the all-powerful Kubō was shrinking rapidly!

From Horigoe Masatomo kept up hostilities against the Koga Kubō throughout the entire period of the Ōnin War. Both claimed to be acting on behalf of the shogun, and both had the unpleasant experience of seeing the Uesugi extend their rule across the region while they squabbled. In 1471 Uesugi forces captured Koga, so Shigeuji had to escape to Chiba, but the fighting continued for thirty years in fruitless attempts to regain the Kantō for the Ashikaga. The Kyōtoku no Ran eventually ceased in 1482, but by that time the situation in the Kantō had changed radically both for the Uesugi and for the rival princes.

The Sengoku Daimyo

There would have been little point in mentioning the long and tedious conflict between the two Kubō and the Uesugi had it not been for the roles they would play as victims of a new breed of provincial lord, because as the shogun's influence waned in the Kantō other powers arrived on the scene as the Sengoku Period began. To a very large extent the Kantō provided its testbed, and as far as the Ashikaga were concerned the new reality would be brought into a particularly sharp focus in the city of Kamakura, which neither Kubō had ever managed to retake from the Uesugi. Instead, one of the new *sengoku daimyo* did just that, and it was achieved in 1512 by a man who was typical of the genre in many ways but who exceeded them all by his cunning and military skill: an up-and-coming leader who would go down in history under the name of Hōjō Sōun (1432–1519), the first of the great *sengoku daimyo* to make his mark upon Japan. Sōun, who lived to be 87, was born during the reign of the first Prince of Kamakura and lived to see the denial of Kamakura to that same princely family three generations later.

The Hōjō would rise from obscurity to dominance of the Kantō over a period of five generations without the need of any favours from shoguns. In 1480 Ise Shinkurō, as Sōun was then known, had only six men under his command. By the time of the death of his great-great grandson in 1590 his original war band had grown to tens of thousands, who defended their territory from formidable castles in the Kantō and only succumbed at the very end to the mighty Toyotomi Hideyoshi, the unifier of Japan. According to one admiring account of Sōun, 'Even when he was an old man his sight and hearing were both undiminished and none of his teeth had fallen out, nor had his dauntlessness changed from when he was in his prime. Sōun impressed everyone because he had raised his family from a genuinely lowly social status'.[7]

The latter sentence may not be entirely true, because humble beginnings have long been assumed for Ise Shinkurō in accordance with his legendary shift from 'rags to riches'. He probably had very respectable family connections; his father is believed to have been an official in the Bakufu who had sufficient means to guarantee his son a good education from the monks of Daitokuji. The Ōnin War was currently raging in Kyoto and Shinkurō, it is thought, accompanied Ashikaga Yoshimi in his escape to Ise, but new horizons opened for Shinkurō when his elder sister married Imagawa Yoshitada, the *shugo* of Suruga Province. Yoshimi returned to Kyoto in 1469, so Shinkurō took the opportunity to move to Suruga and serve his brother-in-law. When Imagawa Yoshitada was killed in battle in 1476 his son Ujichika's rightful inheritance was placed in great peril, so Ise Shinkurō acted as mediator in a dispute that drew in not only the Imagawa retainers but also the Uesugi and the Horigoe Kubō. Shinkurō's diplomatic and military skills settled the matter amicably, for which he received from the grateful heir the reward of the castle of Kōkokuji.

Shinkurō's next acquisition came in a very different way but involved the Horigoe Kubō once again. The first Horigoe Kubō Ashikaga Masatomo died in 1491 and was succeeded by a son who is known to history only by his childhood name of Chachamaru because he never lived long enough to perform his *genbuku* (manhood ceremony). Chachamaru's appointment caused some dissension in Izu Province, so the boy was imprisoned in a small room by his stepmother, but he broke free and killed her. Masatomo's old retainers were horrified by this conduct, so Shinkurō, in a stunning exercise of self-interest, invaded Izu to punish the boy and forced him to commit suicide. The post of Horigoe Kubō was therefore no more, so with the enthusiastic backing of those who had welcomed his intervention, Shinkurō took over Horigoe Castle and added Izu Province to his own territories. He then married his son Ujitsuna (1487–1541) to a descendant of the former Hōjō Regents of Kamakura and took their surname to associate his new and powerful family with those who had once seen off the Mongol Invasions and had fallen foul only to Emperor Go-Daigo. Shinkurō also had his head shaved and assumed the Buddhist name of Sōun.

From that time onwards Sōun went from strength to strength. Most of his success was achieved on the battlefield, where Sōun showed real military genius and seemed to have an uncanny knack of attacking at the right moment. His command of men was also very personal, and Sōun's biographer Miura Jōshin identified strong bonds of loyalty even at the lowest levels of the army. Sōun's ability to attract armed peasants to his banner, to use them effectively and then to gain their loyalty through rewards, places him right at the start of the process that would see ashigaru becoming

---

7   Sugiyama, Hiroshi. 1974. *Sengoku Daimyo*. Tokyo: Chūō Kōronsha, pp.80–81.

THE ROAD TO SENGOKU

the lower ranks of the samurai class.

In 1512 Ujitsuna and his 81-year-old father marched unopposed into Kamakura as part of the Hōjō's strategy to control Sagami Province. To protect his new acquisition Ujitsuna granted tax exemptions to Kamakura's important temples and, showing a strategist's appreciation of the city's historic vulnerability, built Tamanawa Castle to cover its northern approaches. From Tamanawa the Hōjō successfully defended the ancient city for many years to come. In 1526 a daring seaborne raid by the Satomi succeeded in burning down the Tsurugaoka Hachiman Shrine, but Ujitsuna drove the raiders away and killed their leader.[8]

The Hōjō became the undisputed masters of the Kantō over the course of the following few decades, and the Ashikaga princes would be their noblest victims. In 1538 the younger brother of the third Koga Kubō was defeated by Ujitsuna at the first battle of Kōnodai, and in 1545 the fourth Koga Kubō Ashikaga Haruuji was beaten by two of Sōun's grandsons at the epic night battle of Kawagoe. Yet somehow the mystique surrounding the name of Ashikaga allowed the position of Koga Kubō to survive until Hideyoshi's conquest of the Kantō in 1590. The last Koga Kubō would be a woman called Ashikaga Ujinohime (1574–1620), who succeeded to the title in 1583 at the age of nine following the death of her father. In 1590 she was married off and her descendants prospered under the Tokugawa.

Hōjō Sōun (1432–1519) was the first of the great *sengoku daimyo* to make his mark upon Japan. In this illustration he is shown attacking Horigoe Castle and destroying the last Horigoe Kubō.

---

8   Hagiwara, T (Ed.) 1966. *Hōjō Godai ki* in *Hōjō shiryō shu*. (*Sengoku Shiryō Sōsho Vol. 1*) Tokyo: Jinbutsu Ōraisha, p.252.

THE ŌNIN WAR

As for the Koga Kubō's great rivals the Uesugi, their fortunes would become so reduced by the Hōjō and other enemies that in 1551 they were forced to adopt one of their own vassals to ensure that the name continued. He became Uesugi Kenshin (1530–1578) and would challenge the Hōjō for supremacy in Eastern Japan with little reference to the now largely irrelevant power of the shogun in Kyoto or his princely representatives. Yet the magic of the old titles linked to the shogun still lived on, and in 1561 Kenshin stood in front of the Tsurugaoka Shrine in Kamakura to proclaim himself as the new Kantō Kanrei, the exalted (if now meaningless) rank enjoyed by the Uesugi of old.[9] Within months Kenshin would be fighting for his very existence at the fierce battle of Kawanakajima against an enemy like himself. The Sengoku Period was now in full swing, and the very different circumstances under which the Ōnin War had been conducted had already become a distant memory.

---

9   Tamiya, Yukio. 1977. *Yonezawa hanso Uesugi Kenshin*. Yonezawa: Endo Shoten, p.90.

Bibliography

Ackroyd, Joyce (Trans.). 1982. *Lessons from History: Arai Hakuseki's Tokushi yoron.* St. Lucia: University of Queensland Press.

Berry, Mary Elizabeth. 1994. *The culture of Civil War in Kyoto.* Berkeley: University of California Press.

Conlan, Thomas D. 2010. 'Instruments of Change: Organisational Technology and the Consolidation of Regional Power in Japan, 1333–1600', in Ferejohn, John A. & Rosenbluth, Frances McCall (Eds.). *War and State Building in Medieval Japan*: 124–158. Stanford: Stanford University Press, pp.124–158.

Conlan, Thomas D. 2020. 'The "Ōnin War" as the Fulfilment of Prophecy' *The Journal of Japanese Studies*, 46, 1, pp.31–60.

Davis, David L. 1974 'Ikki in Late Medieval Japan' in Hall, John W. & Mass, Jeffrey P. *Medieval Japan: Essays in Institutional History.* Stanford: Stanford University Press, pp.221–147.

Eikyō ki http://muromachi.movie.coocan.jp/eikyouki/eikyouki05.html (Accessed 21 April 2020).

Goza, Yūichi. 2016. *Ōnin no Ran: Sengoku jidai o undo tairan.* Tokyo: Chūō Kōronsha.

Hagiwara, T (Ed.) 1966. *Hōjō Godai ki* in *Hōjō shiryō shu.* (*Sengoku Shiryō Sōsho Vol. 1*) Tokyo: Jinbutsu Ōraisha.

Hall, John W. & Toyoda, Takeshi (Eds.). 1977. *Japan in the Muromachi Age.* Berkeley: University of California Press.

Hanawa Hokiichi. 1912. *Gunsho Ruijū* Vol 13 (1912 edition) (Tokyo: Publisher unknown).

Hayashiya, Tatsusaburō. 1977. 'Kyoto in the Muromachi Age', in Hall, John W. & Toyoda, Takeshi (Eds.) *Japan in the Muromachi Age.* Berkeley: University of California Press, pp.15–36.

Ishinomori, Shōtarō. 2017a. *Dōmin, Bakufu wo yurugasu.* Tokyo: Chūō Kōronsha.

Ishinomori, Shōtarō. 2017b. *Ōhō-fubō no hametsu – Ōnin no Ran.* Tokyo: Chūō Kōronsha,

Izawa Motohiko 2003. *Gyakusetsu no Nihonshi: Muromachi Bunka to Ikki no Nazo.* Tokyo: Shogakkan.

Kanda, Chisato. 2002. *Nihon no Chūsei: Sengoku ransei wo ikiru kata.* Tokyo: Chūō Kōronsha.

Keene, Donald. 2003. *Yoshimasa and the Silver Pavilion: The Creation of the Soul of Japan*. New York: Columbia University Press.
Minegishi, Sumio. 2017. *Kyōtoku no Ran*. Tokyo: Kōdansha.
Murdoch, Sir James. 1925. *A History of Japan Volume I*. (2nd Impression). London: Kegan Paul, Trench and Trubner.
Nakanishi, Ritta. 1985. 'Hassekiboku' *Rekishi Gunzō*, 17, 2, pp.82–85.
Nakanishi, Ritta. 2008. *Nihon katchū shi*. Tokyo: Dainippon Kaiga.
Nakashima, Atsumi. 2016. *Ninja o kagaku suru*. Tokyo: Yōsensha.
Needham, Joseph. 1986. *Science and Civilisation in China, Vol. 5 Part 7 Military Technology; the Gunpowder Epic*. Cambridge: Cambridge University Press.
Ogawa, Makoto. 2013. *Yamana Sōzen to Hosokawa Katsumoto*. Tokyo: Yoshikawa Kōbunkan.
Saitō Toshio, et al. 1981. *Ikki (2) Ikki no Rekishi*. Tokyo: Tokyo University Press.
Sansom, George. 1961. *A History of Japan: 1334–1615*. London: The Cresset Press.
Shimizu, Noboru. 2008. *Sengoku ninja retsuden*. Tokyo: Kawade Shobo Shinsha.
Shimura, Kunihiro. 2017. *Ōnin ki*. Tokyo: Chikuma Shobō.
Stavros, Matthew. 2006. 'Building Warrior Legitimacy in Medieval Kyoto'. *East Asian History*, 31, pp.1–28.
Sugiyama, Hiroshi. 1974. *Sengoku Daimyo*. Tokyo: Chūō Kōronsha.
Suzuki, Masaya. 2001. *Nazo toki Nihon kassen shi: Nihonjin wa dō tatakatte kita ka*. Tokyo: Kōdansha.
Tamiya, Yukio. 1977. *Yonezawa hanso Uesugi Kenshin*. Yonezawa: Endō Shoten.
Tōma, Shi'ichi. 1994. 'Hiya ni tsuite'. *Nantō ko-ko* 14, pp.123–152.
Turnbull, S.R. 1977. *The Samurai: A Military History*. London: Osprey.
Uezato, Takashi. 2000. 'Ryūkyū no kaki ni tsuite'. *Okinawa Bunka* 36, 1, pp.73–92.
Unsen, Taikyoku: *Hekizan Nichiroku* (2017 edition). *Hekizan Nichiroku Vol. 2* Edited by Tokyo Daigaku Shiryō Hensanjo. Tokyo: Iwanami Shoten.
Various Authors. 1994. *Ōnin no Ran* (Rekishi Gunzō Series 37) Tokyo: Gakken
Various authors. 2006. *Hosokawa Katsumoto: Yamana Sōzen to Ōnin no Ran*. (Nihon no Kassen Series Vol. 48). Tokyo: Kodansha.
Varley, H. Paul. 1967. *The Ōnin War* New York: Columbia University Press.
Yashiro, Kazuo 1994 *Akamatsu Monogatari: Kakitsu ki*. Tokyo, Bensei.